Marital Settlement and Joint Parenting Agreements Line by Line

A Detailed Look at Marital Settlement and Joint Parenting Agreements and How to Draft Them to Meet Your Clients' Needs

Stan R. Weller

ASPATORE

Project Manager, Kristen Lindeman; edited by Melanie Zimmerman; proofread by Jo Alice Darden

ISBN 978-0-314-27682-7

For corrections, updates, comments, or any other inquiries, please e-mail
TLR.AspatoreEditorial@thomson.com.

First Printing, 2011
10 9 8 7 6 5 4 3 2 1

Mat #41176261

ASPATORE

Aspatore Books, a Thomson Reuters business, exclusively publishes C-Level executives (CEO, CFO, CTO, CMO, Partner) from the world's most respected companies and law firms. C-Level Business Intelligence™, as conceptualized and developed by Aspatore Books, provides professionals of all levels with proven business intelligence from industry insiders—direct and unfiltered insight from those who know it best—as opposed to third-party accounts offered by unknown authors and analysts. Aspatore Books is committed to publishing an innovative line of business and legal books, those which lay forth principles and offer insights that, when employed, can have a direct financial impact on the reader's business objectives, whatever they may be. In essence, Aspatore publishes critical tools for all business professionals.

DEDICATION

This book is dedicated to:

My parents, Stephen and Jeanette Weller, who taught me what a family is.

My son, Quinlan Weller, who taught me what being a father is.

My wife, Angela Weller, who taught me what love is.

CONTENTS

Introduction

The marital settlement agreement, joint parenting agreement, and other documents set forth in the appendices and discussed herein are designed for the family law practitioner, general practice attorney, paralegal, mediator, and law student. As such, each section in this book will outline several alternatives in drafting these settlement agreements. The documents provided are not designed to be all-inclusive, but rather provide a suitable starting point for the drafting of documents to be entered in conjunction with a final, enforceable court order. A proposed final order is provided in Appendix D, setting forth language to incorporate the marital settlement agreement and joint parenting agreement as independent but inclusive documentation.

The goal of any marital settlement agreement is to define the terms and conditions of settlement and resolve any loose ends that may remain as part of the dissolution of marriage process. Ideally, the parties will not have to return to the court for either clarification or enforcement.

Likewise, the goal of any joint parenting agreement is to define the responsibilities, terms, conditions, and priorities of the parents in jointly parenting the parties' minor children. Practitioners and parties alike are advised to keep in mind the best interest of the children in any such agreement.

This book is divided into two parts. The first part focuses on the marital settlement agreement (MSA). The MSA should serve to resolve all financial issues between the parties and incorporate financial resolutions regarding minor children. The specific elements or paragraphs of the marital settlement agreement to be addressed are:

MARITAL SETTLEMENT AGREEMENT
- 1.0   Maintenance
- 2.0   Real Estate
- 3.0   Marital Property
- 4.0   Personal Property

The second part of this book focuses on the joint parenting agreement (JPA). The JPA should serve to resolve all issues regarding the minor children (except financial). The specific elements or paragraphs of the JPA are:

JOINT PARENTING AGREEMENT

The sections in both the MSA and the JPA are not the ingredients of a recipe, but rather the interlocking pieces of a puzzle. As such, it is hoped that the information provided in this book is first used proactively to give definition to the underlying agreement, and then to provide possibilities for fleshing out all remaining issues.

Whether you are a paralegal using the facts and information provided in creating a first draft of settlement documents, an attorney completing a final agreement, or a mediator attempting initial settlement, the MSA, JPA, and final order provided should be of vital assistance in the completion of a dissolution of marriage. After all, a divorce is ultimately a line-by-line division of all debts, assets, and responsibilities.

The following line-by-line analysis contains the language for a Marital Settlement Agreement and Joint Parenting Agreement in bold type, with a brief explanatory description following each section. Alternative provisions to consider including are presented in bold italics. The appendix contains a complete form of a Marital Settlement Agreement, Joint Parenting Agreement, and Final Order.

Line-by-Line Analysis:
Marital Settlement Agreement

MARITAL SETTLEMENT AGREEMENT

This Agreement is entered into on the date set forth below by and between the Plaintiff, Rose Smith, hereinafter referred to as "Wife," and the Respondent, Richard Smith, hereinafter referred to as "Husband."

Identification of Parties

The marital settlement agreement (MSA) begins by identifying the parties. In the example herein, the parties are the fictitious, but infamous, Rose and Richard Smith. Sparing the details of the derailed marriage, Rose will be the plaintiff throughout the MSA and the joint parenting agreement (JPA) discussed in Part II.

Both the plaintiff and the defendant are identified initially by name and thereafter by either "wife" or "husband." Although such monikers do not sound as artfully pled throughout the agreement as "plaintiff" and "defendant," such designations lend readability to the document for the litigants during negotiations, as well as for later reference months and years after the entry of these agreements.

WITNESSETH:

WHEREAS:

A. There is a current dissolution of marriage proceeding pending under Case Number ____-D-____, entitled "<u>In re the Marriage of Rose Smith vs. Richard Smith</u>," and no Final Order has yet been entered in that case.

B. Both parties consider it to be in their best interest
to settle between themselves all issues that are
currently pending in this matter which arise out of
the marital relationship or any other relationship
between the parties, including all rights of every
kind and nature, whether marital or non-marital,
real, personal or mixed, which either of them now
has or may later claim to have against the other;
the right of either party to receive maintenance,
and the payment of attorney's fees and costs.

Recitals

The above paragraphs are not just the typical "WHEREAS" boilerplate
recitals setting forth proper consideration of a contract. These
alphabetically enumerated paragraphs are necessary and vital dicta for both
the parties, as well as for the attorney or draftsman of the agreement.

Paragraphs A and B are the general consideration language and the
indication of a desire to resolve all issues. Parties should be reminded that
this document, like any other legal contract, is subject to the "four corner"
theory of contract enforcement, and anything not explicitly included should
be considered excluded. The MSA should be given the legal weight and
consideration any other contract or settlement document would be given in
any other legal context, family law or otherwise.

C. This Agreement is made free of collusion and is
not made for the purpose of obtaining or
stimulating a dissolution of marriage of the
parties; however, the parties stipulate and agree
that the dissolution of marriage proceedings now
pending in the court aforesaid shall proceed and
be heard as an uncontested matter as soon as
practicable. The Husband hereby enters his
appearance in the above-entitled cause as
Defendant   therein and expressly waives the
necessity of process of summons and consents
that the same proceedings may be had herein as

> **fully and with the same force and effect as though he had been duly and regularly served with process of summons therein in the State of Illinois at least thirty (30) days prior to any return date designated by Plaintiff herein or as otherwise provided by law.**

Entry of Appearance

After a client understands the consequence of the MSA, a useful device of the agreement is the incorporation of the entry of appearance and consent to judgment set forth in Paragraph C, above. Although certain jurisdictions have more thorough or comprehensive entries of appearance or consents to judgment, the language above has been routinely accepted in the state of Illinois. Obviously, the individual practitioner must comply with the requirements of the corresponding jurisdiction.

An additional benefit to the client may be the avoidance of additional court fees. By incorporation of the entry of appearance into the MSA, a party may avoid the entry fee or answer fee in certain jurisdictions.

If a separate entry of appearance is required or has already been filed, or if additional forms are necessary, Paragraph C can be abbreviated to:

> **C. *This Agreement is not made for the purpose of obtaining or stimulating a dissolution of marriage of the parties; however, the parties stipulate and agree that the dissolution of marriage proceedings now pending in the court aforesaid shall proceed and be heard as an uncontested matter.***

> **D. Each party acknowledges and understands that they have the right to conduct discovery, including, but not limited to; conducting depositions, submitting interrogatories, requesting the production of documents, and a mental or physical examination of the opposing party. Both parties have full knowledge and understanding of**

the finances of this marriage, including property, liabilities and income. Both parties waive their right to conduct formal discovery in an effort to expedite these proceedings and minimize the expenses associated with this case.

Discovery Waiver

Paragraph D explains with specificity that discovery has not been completed, by agreement of the parties. Incorporation of this paragraph is vital to the protection of the parties and the attorneys. Obviously, this paragraph is necessary only if discovery has not already been completed.

E. Each party has had the opportunity to consult with his or her own attorney and each party acknowledges that he or she is not relying upon advice provided by counsel in evaluating the provisions of this Agreement. Each party expressly states that neither have given or received any promises or considerations other than those set forth herein. Both parties expressly state that they have freely and voluntarily entered into this Agreement free of any duress and coercion with full knowledge of each and every provision, and the consequences thereof.

NOW, THEREFORE, in consideration of the mutual and several promises and undertakings contained herein and for other good and valuable consideration, the receipt and sufficiency of which is mutually acknowledged, the parties do hereby agree as follows.

Acknowledgement

Paragraph E sets forth that the parties are voluntarily entering into this agreement over and above the explicit advice of the attorney(s) and is admittedly self-serving for the drafter. Finally, the last paragraph is the parties' request for acceptance and admittance into the judgment of dissolution.

ARTICLE 1
MAINTENANCE

1.1   In consideration of the various promises, agreements and conditions contained in this Agreement, the Wife hereby waives any and all rights she may have to maintenance from the Husband, past, present and future, pursuant to the laws of the State of Illinois or of any other state or country. The Wife acknowledges that this waiver forever bars her from asserting a claim for maintenance against the Husband.

1.2   In consideration of the various promises, agreements and conditions contained in this Agreement, the Husband hereby waives any and all rights he may have to maintenance from the Wife, past, present and future, pursuant to the laws of the State of Illinois or of any other state or country. The Husband acknowledges that this waiver forever bars him from asserting a claim for maintenance against the Wife.

Article 1: Maintenance

Maintenance, formerly known as alimony, is typically an issue best addressed early in the dialogue of settlement (or contest). Whether maintenance is an issue can frame or outline many of the remaining issues of property division, retirement division, or business interests. Assuming a comprehensive settlement, the drafter need only set forth the agreement, not explain it. In any event, maintenance must be addressed to prevent later contestation.

In the examples, language always includes both parties to account for the interests of both parties. The first example, above, a simple bilateral waiver, is set forth. Most jurisdictions require a specific waiver to allay any future claims for maintenance.

In the second example, below, temporary or rehabilitative maintenance language is set forth for the wife. Temporary maintenance is typically limited by time or a specific event. In some negotiations, a client will request a specific event occur before maintenance terminates, such as obtaining a bachelor's degree. Such a potentially elusive achievement should be avoided. A party may be unable to attain a bachelor's degree because of lack of initiative (after all, maintenance will continue until completed), lack of ability, or even a situation outside of the recipient's control (such as illness). Instead, a time-specific termination is to be favored. Additionally, it may be advisable to either retain or exclude the typical statutory maintenance terminating language, such as remarriage, cohabitation, and so on. By setting forth that the maintenance shall continue for a specific time, regardless of any "typical" or statutorily terminating event, the recipient party will be protected and hopefully able to "rehabilitate" himself or herself to adequately provide for himself or herself, regardless of other future events. See Paragraph 1.1 below. Also included below in Paragraph 1.2 is the husband's waiver of any claim to maintenance against the wife.

Finally, the remaining example below is that of permanent maintenance with terminal language. It should be noted that awards of permanent maintenance are becoming more atypical. Careful consideration should be given before including an award of permanent maintenance, which should be used only after all potential temporary maintenance options are exhausted.

(TEMPORARY-REHABILITATIVE MAINTENANCE)

1.1   The Wife shall be awarded temporary maintenance in the amount of $800.00 (eight hundred dollars) per month, commencing the first month after the entry of the dissolution of marriage, payable on the 1st of each month thereafter. Payments shall terminate after 48 monthly installment payments of the above referenced amount, or in the event of the Wife's death, remarriage, cohabitation (conjugal) with another person on a regular basis, or upon any other statutorily defined event.   ALTERNATIVELY:

Payments shall terminate after 48 monthly installments irregardless of remarriage, cohabitation (conjugal) with another person on a regular basis, or any other statutorily defined event to provide for the financial rehabilitation of the Wife.

1.2   In consideration of the various promises, agreements and conditions contained in this Agreement, the Husband hereby waives any and all rights he may have to maintenance from the Wife, past, present and future, pursuant to the laws of the State of Illinois or of any other state or country. The Husband acknowledges that this waiver forever bars his from asserting a claim for maintenance against the Wife.

(PERMANENT MAINTENANCE)

1.1   The Wife shall be awarded permanent maintenance in the amount of $800.00 (eight hundred dollars) per month, commencing the first month after the entry of the dissolution of marriage, payable on the 1st of each month thereafter. Payments shall terminate in the event of the Wife's death, remarriage, cohabitation (on a conjugal basis) with another person on a regular basis, or upon any other statutorily defined event.

1.2   In consideration of the various promises, agreements and conditions contained in this Agreement, the Husband hereby waives any and all rights he may have to maintenance from the Wife, past, present and future, pursuant to the laws of the State of Illinois or of any other state or country. The Husband acknowledges that this waiver forever bars his from asserting a claim for maintenance against the Wife.

As a final note, maintenance is not dischargeable in bankruptcy. 11 U.S.C. §
523. Any client who agrees to settlement that includes maintenance or a
settlement of debt or assets "In Lieu of Maintenance" should be apprised
of the bankruptcy bar to discharge. Additionally, specific note must be
taken of Section 8.0 below regarding bankruptcy, and said section(s) should
be modified accordingly.

ARTICLE 2
REAL ESTATE

**2.1   The Husband shall be awarded, as his sole
and exclusive property, the marital home at 1600
Pennsylvania Ave. HomeTown, Illinois and shall
assume responsibility for the indebtedness owed
thereon and shall hold harmless the Wife on such
indebtedness. Further, he shall pay all mortgage
payments in a timely manner until refinance. He shall
transfer all utilities solely into his name and shall pay
same. The Husband shall be responsible for all real
estate bills levied against the property, existing or as
to be billed in the future.**

**2.2   The Husband shall refinance or assume the
mortgage on such that the Wife is no longer on any
mortgage or indebtedness on said property within one
year of the entry of dissolution of marriage. The Wife
shall execute a quit claim deed conveying her interest
to the Husband to remove her name from said
property concurrent with any sale, refinance or
assumption of the mortgage.**

**2.3   In the event Husband fails to refinance the
indebtedness so as to remove Wife's name from the
indebtedness thereon within one year, or in the event
Husband fails to timely pay the mortgage payments,
the marital home shall be immediately listed for sale
and sold as soon as possible. Upon sale of the marital
home the parties shall equally divide the proceeds (or**

divide equally any deficiency/loss) of the sale after any reasonable and customary closing costs, realtor fees and outstanding mortgages have been paid.

2.4   Unless the parties agree or a court orders otherwise, the property shall not be sold for less than a sum sufficient to cover all mortgages and costs of the sale. The parties shall agree on a real estate agent to list the property. In the event the parties cannot agree on a real estate agent, then they shall each select one real estate agent and those two agents shall confer and select a third real estate agent who will list the property for sale. The parties shall agree on the initial listing price and any reductions in the listing price. However, if the parties cannot agree, the listing agent shall make the decision as to any reductions in the listing price. If an offer to buy is made and the parties cannot agree on whether to accept the offer, they may petition the court for resolution of the issue. The parties shall cooperate to execute any documents necessary to effectuate any of the provisions of this section regarding the marital home.

Article 2: Real Estate

The marital real estate typically holds the most intrinsic value, if not the most economic value, of a dissolution proceeding. However the home is divided, it is imperative that all potential outcomes be addressed to eliminate the lingering effects of the mortgage and incidents of ownership to one or both parties.

First, the actual title conveyance must be addressed. The "sole and exclusive" owner of the property does not want to have to track down the co-owner (former spouse) to effectuate a sale or transfer of the property years after the entry of dissolution of marriage. Additionally, because of the residual effect of a deed held in joint tenancy, there is a potential for liability if a surviving ex-spouse were to suddenly inherit a property.

Second, the now "non-owner" of property needs to be absolved of his or her indebtedness on the outstanding mortgage. The family court has jurisdiction with regard only to the parties and not to the mortgage company. The court cannot force a mortgage company to refinance a property or give credit to an individual who does not otherwise qualify. Therefore, any enforceability clause must incorporate alternative relief for the parties.

Finally, if the property is to be sold outright (or as a last resort), all potential sale options should be included to forestall further litigation. In the example above, most of the possibilities are addressed via a full award of the property to one of the parties. In this case, the husband, Richard, is receiving the marital home, provided he can refinance said property and continue to make all mortgage payments on time. If he fails to refinance or otherwise comply with the terms listed, the wife may avail herself of the listed remedies.

In the example above, the house is being awarded to one of the parties. As a matter of practice, there are three conventional options when dividing an ownership of a residence:

1) The property is awarded to one of the parties, as set forth above.
2) The property is sold, and the proceeds and/or losses are divided equally.
3) The property is surrendered in a bankruptcy.

As a matter of course, the first option is the most detailed. In addition to the specifics of the refinance and assumption of all incidents of ownership of the property, as well as the terms and conditions for a sale in the event of a breach of the agreed terms, the parties may have substantial equity in the real property. If there are insufficient other marital assets to offset the equity, Paragraph 2.2 may be written to include refinance of the property with part of the equity being paid to the other spouse.

ALTERNATIVE PROVISION

2.2   The Husband shall refinance or assume the mortgage on such that the Wife is no longer on any mortgage or indebtedness on said property within one year of the entry of dissolution of marriage. Said refinance shall be in an amount sufficient to pay off all existing mortgages and to include funds sufficient to pay to the Wife the sum of thirty-five thousand dollars ($35,000.00) as and for her portion of the marital equity in the property. The Wife shall execute a quit claim deed conveying her interest to the Husband to remove her name from said property concurrent with any sale, refinance or assumption of the mortgage.

If the parties cannot otherwise agree to award the property to one or the other, the property can be sold. Additionally, in today's world, a marital home is often the product of a two-income household. As such, it is not unusual to have to sell the home because, as individuals, the parties can neither pay the mortgage nor obtain financing individually, no matter their creditworthiness. If the real estate is to be sold, definitive language as to the procedure should be included, as set forth below.

ALTERNATIVE PROVISIONS

2.1   The marital home located at 1600 Pennsylvania Ave. HomeTown, Illinois shall be immediately listed for sale and sold as soon as possible. Upon sale of the marital home the parties shall equally divide the proceeds (or divide equally any deficiency/loss) of the sale after any reasonable and customary closing costs, realtor fees and outstanding mortgages have been paid.

2.2   Unless the parties agree or a court orders otherwise, the property shall not be sold for less than a sum sufficient to cover all mortgages and costs of the sale. The parties shall agree on a real estate agent to list the property. In the event the parties cannot agree on a real estate agent, then they shall each select one real estate agent and those two agents shall confer and select a third real estate agent who will list the property for sale. The parties shall agree on the initial listing price and any reductions in the listing price. However, if the parties cannot agree, the listing agent shall make the decision as to any reductions in the listing price. If an offer to buy is made and the parties cannot agree on whether to accept the offer, they may petition the court for resolution of the issue. The parties shall cooperate to execute any documents necessary to effectuate any of the provisions of this section regarding the marital home.

Finally, if the property is to be surrendered in bankruptcy, it should be so stated. An asset with issues of title, liens, and potential foreclosure litigation should not be left out merely because bankruptcy is the anticipated action of one or both parties. Further, current possession issues should be addressed.

ALTERNATIVE PROVISIONS

2.1   The parties currently own the marital residence located at 1600 Pennsylvania Ave. HomeTown, Illinois that is to be surrendered in bankruptcy as is anticipated to be filed by both parties. The Husband shall maintain temporary possession of the residence until the property is properly surrendered in bankruptcy. Neither party shall maintain any responsibility for any debt owed thereon nor maintain any ownership interest therein.

2.2   Both parties shall comply with all requirements of the bankruptcy proceedings with regards to the marital home and shall cooperate with any requests of the bankruptcy trustee(s) and mortgage company representatives.

Any other property—rental, investment, or pleasure—can be divided using substantially the same formulas as provided above. Similarly, if the property was premarital property, said property should be so designated and awarded accordingly.

Article 3: Marital Property

Marital property is usually defined as all property, realty or personalty, that was obtained or earned during the marriage. However, in attempting to create a comprehensive and clear settlement document, it is best to provide a separate section for any item not easily disposed of between the parties. Already addressed is the marital home/real estate, above. Likewise, additional sections later set forth such items as financial accounts, vehicles, and so on. This leaves the attorney with the catch-all section of "marital property."

If you are reading this book, you have the luxury of dealing with parties who have been able to negotiate all aspects of the dissolution process. In many instances, this marital property section is the least problematic. If the parties have already separated and have divided the tangible "spoils of war," each party need only be awarded such property in his or her own possession. Simple, effective language is provided in the first example, below.

ARTICLE 3
MARITAL PROPERTY

3.1   **The Husband shall be awarded all marital property (not otherwise referenced in this Marital Settlement Agreement) now in his possession as his sole and exclusive property.**

3.2   **The Wife shall be awarded all marital property (not otherwise referenced in this Marital Settlement Agreement) now in her possession as her sole and exclusive property.**

If the parties are not yet separated, or additional specific division is required, a comprehensive division is necessary. However, a truly comprehensive list is virtually impossible. As such, a comprehensive list for only one party is advisable and typically much more workable.

Bear in mind that a comprehensive list should be just that—comprehensive. Many parties have substantially duplicate items; therefore, any item(s) listed should be described with sufficient specificity to identify the particular item.

In the example below, Rose is provided a finite list of property that she must remove by a specified date. Since Richard is maintaining possession of the home, it is more efficient to list the items she is taking with her. All other items will remain in the house as the husband's sole and exclusive property. By limiting the time for which the recipient may retrieve her items, the other party is not obligated to await pickup (and otherwise maintain care and control of said items) indefinitely.

MARITAL PROPERTY – specific items

3.1   The Husband shall be awarded all marital property (not otherwise referenced in this Marital Settlement Agreement) now in his possession except the items set forth in paragraph 3.2 below.

3.2   The Wife shall be awarded the following items currently located in the marital residence:

> *a.   King sized bed and mattress and the matching furniture located in the master bedroom.*
>
> *b.   Formal Dining Room Set (table, 6 chairs, and accessories)*
>
> *c.   Small brown dresser (located in guest bedroom)*
>
> *d.   Oak Hutch*
>
> *e.   Riding lawn mower*
>
> *f .   The wedding china (floral pattern)*

> *g.*   *The couch, love seat and end tables from the formal living room*
> *h.*   *DVD / Surround sound system*
> *i.*   *The Sony 32 inch flat panel television*
> *j.*   *The T-Fal cookware set*
> *k.*   *The washer and dryer*
> *l.*   *All wall hangings/decorations*
> *m.*   *A digital copy of all marital/family photos*

All items listed above shall be removed from the martial residence within 30 days of the entry of dissolution of marriage. The Husband shall cooperate and assist the Wife in removing said items. Any items not specifically listed above shall remain in the residence and shall be the exclusive property of the Husband. In the event the items listed above have not been removed within the allotted 30 days, said items shall also be deemed to be the sole and exclusive property of the Husband.

Finally, the parties may have waived maintenance in Section 1.0 above, yet may otherwise divide assets or debts "in Lieu of Maintenance," and such designation need only be added to the above example. Alternatively, this section may be used in conjunction with an award of temporary maintenance to offset the necessity of permanent maintenance. For example, if there are sufficient liquid assets or tangible items, a lion's share of such assets can be awarded to a party to achieve an "equitable" division.

ARTICLE 4
PERSONAL PROPERTY

4.1   **The Husband shall be awarded all personal property (not otherwise referenced in this Marital Settlement Agreement) now in his possession as his sole and exclusive property.**

4.2   The Wife shall be awarded all personal property (not otherwise referenced in this Marital Settlement Agreement) now in her possession as her sole and exclusive property.

Article 4: Personal Property

Personal property or non-marital property is typically defined as items owned before the marriage, gifts, inheritance, and personal items, such as clothes and accessories.

In many instances, this personal property section is substantially similar to the marital property section above. If the parties have already separated and are in possession of their respective items, each party needs to be awarded only such property in his or her possession. The same simple, yet effective language from the marital property section above is provided in the first example above. Otherwise, an attorney should incorporate the comprehensive list approach, as previously discussed.

ARTICLE 5
VEHICLES

5.1   The Wife shall be awarded the 2003 Jeep Wrangler and the 2006 Coleman Camper as her sole and exclusive possession and shall assume responsibility for the indebtedness owed thereon and shall hold harmless the Husband on such indebtedness. The Wife shall refinance and re-title said vehicles within six (6) months of the entry of dissolution of marriage removing the Husband from any incidents of ownership thereon.

5.2   The Husband shall be awarded the 2004 Ford F150 and the 2007 Triumph Rocket III as his sole and exclusive possession and shall assume responsibility for the indebtedness owed thereon and shall hold harmless the Husband on such indebtedness. The Husband shall refinance and re-title said vehicles

within six (6) months of the entry of dissolution of marriage removing the Wife from any incidents of ownership thereon.

5.3   Each party shall sign all necessary documents, titles or loan documents to effectuate the transfer and refinance of the above referenced vehicles.

Article 5: Vehicles

As discussed previously, there are catchall provisions for all property, marital and non-marital (Sections 3.0 and 4.0 above), that account for all items except those not otherwise set forth in specific categories. "Vehicles" is such a category that bears independent mention. Vehicles, like the other items that warrant independent categories, are potentially a combination of marital and non-marital property. Instead of identifying that one vehicle is marital and another is non-marital (and accounting for them in separate categories), it is easier to list the agreed division than explain it.

In the example above, all vehicles are listed and awarded to the respective parties. It is typical to include in this category every item with a title, such as a camper or a motorcycle. Language is included to account for title transfer, as well as refinance. Additional language as to the sale of an item in the event of inability to refinance may also be included. As a matter of practice, sale provisions are not included primarily because such loans are of short duration. The parties' respective income and likelihood of refinance should be addressed in the negotiations. It is seldom advisable to allow an award of an item to a party that he or she clearly cannot afford, thus leaving the other party potentially liable therefor.

However, if bankruptcy is a potential solution for one or both parties, additional language should account for this contingency. Throughout this book, various references have been made to bankruptcy wherein both parties have filed or will be filing bankruptcy. In this example, language is specific to the bankruptcy for only one of the parties. In an effort to reduce redundancy in this and prior examples, this is the only example making such a distinction. However, similar language can be substituted throughout your MSA.

ALTERNATIVE PROVISION

5.1   The Wife shall be awarded the 2008 Toyota Solara as her sole and exclusive property. She shall assume responsibility of all indebtedness thereon and hold harmless and husband of such indebtedness. The Husband shall sign all necessary paperwork to affect the transfer of the vehicle into the Wife's sole ownership.

5.2   The Husband shall be awarded sole possession of the 2007 Ford Explorer which is subject to the party's current bankruptcy. The Husband shall surrender the vehicle pursuant to the bankruptcy requirements and both parties shall take all necessary steps as required by the bankruptcy court, trustee and lien holder to affect the surrender of said vehicle.

5.3   Both parties shall cooperate with regards to any requirements with the bankruptcy court to enable the Wife to maintain possession of the vehicle listed in section 5.1 above.

Debts

The issue of marital debt and personal debt is similar to the issues of marital property and personal property discussed previously. Marital debt is typically debt incurred during the marriage. Some of these debts are secured and as such are addressed specifically by the award of the item(s) securing those debts (such as set forth in Sections 2.0 and 5.0, above). The remaining marital debt is resolved in sections 6.0 and 7.0, below.

ARTICLE 6
MARITAL DEBTS

6.1   The Wife shall assume responsibility for all indebtedness owed in her name and she shall hold harmless the Husband on such indebtedness.

6.2   The Husband shall assume responsibility for all indebtedness owed in his name and he shall hold harmless the Wife on such indebtedness.

6.3   There are no jointly held marital debts.

Article 6: Marital Debts

All marital debts not otherwise divided or accounted for in the other sections of the MSA should be assigned in this section.

Often, in short-term marriages, the parties have not consolidated debt or obtained jointly held unsecured debt. As long as the balances held by each party are consistent with an equitable division (or a division the parties can accept), it is often possible to divide the liability subject to the debts in his or her individual name. In so doing, neither party has any continuing financial ties to the other. Such a simple division is set forth above.

Additionally, if the parties have been separated for a period sufficient to bring into question any financial activity the other is unaware of, it is advisable to add language to hold liable the party incurring such debt after the date of separation. After all, Rose will likely be unwilling to pay half of any debt incurred by Richard while entertaining his paramour, even though such debt, by definition, may be a marital debt.

OPTIONAL PROVISION

6.4   Each party shall be solely responsible to pay any and all debts and liabilities which he or she has incurred since the date (insert date) of the parties' separation, any debts secured by any property awarded to that party and all debts in his or her own name, including debts not named herein. Each party shall indemnify and hold the other harmless from or against any liability for those debts, including the payment of the other's attorney's fees and costs associated with the default on any such debt.

If the parties have jointly held debt, or the duration of the marriage draws into question the contractual liability for the parties' debt, it is advisable to take the steps necessary to verify same. Once definitive contractual liability is established, it is advisable to divide as much of the individually held marital debt by the debt holder as possible. By doing so, each party will not later be sought out for collection if the ex-spouse fails in his or her duties to pay such debt. Although language should always be added that a non-paying spouse indemnify and hold harmless the other spouse, enforcement and reimbursement will be found in the marital court, not the court handling the collections.

Any debt that cannot otherwise be divided by contract liability must be clearly identified and the responsibility defined. Additionally, if a division is made "in lieu of maintenance," the parties should be advised of the non-dischargeablity repercussions for the payer spouse if he or she files bankruptcy. In the example below, language regarding both possibilities is included.

ALTERNATIVE PROVISION

6.1   The Wife shall assume responsibility for all indebtedness owed in her name, except the debts set forth in paragraph 6.2 below, and she shall hold harmless the Husband on such indebtedness.

6.2   The Husband shall assume responsibility for all indebtedness owed in his name and the jointly held marital debts, namely:

> *a)   The CitiBank Visa account ending 4545*
> *b)   The Bank of America MasterCard account ending 7878*
> *c)   The Home Depot account ending 1010*

The debts set forth in paragraph a, b, and c above are in lieu of maintenance and shall not be dischargeable in bankruptcy. The Husband shall indemnify and hold harmless the Wife on the indebtedness set forth herein.

Debts awarded in lieu of maintenance are rare, so the sentence immediately following the enumerated debts should be included only in such rare occasions. The remaining language, however, would remain unchanged.

ARTICLE 7
PERSONAL DEBTS

7.1   The Husband shall be responsible for all debts currently in his name, including his student loans, and shall hold harmless the Wife on such indebtedness.

7.2   The Wife shall be responsible for all debts currently in her name and shall hold harmless the Husband on such indebtedness.

Article 7: Personal Debts

Personal debts are typically debts incurred prior to the marriage or as part of a complex set of circumstances setting such debts apart from the typical marital debt. One such example is that of student loans. Nevertheless, in drafting an *agreed* MSA, these issues should be resolved or moot, and a simple statement of responsibilities for personal debt need only be included. But such a paragraph must be included to make the MSA fully comprehensive.

ARTICLE 8
BANKRUPTCY

8.1   Both parties agree and understand that either party may file bankruptcy. In the event that either party (or both) file bankruptcy, neither party shall be bound by the terms of indemnification as set forth herein. Both parties agree to cooperate with any bankruptcy court or trustee and each other regarding a bankruptcy filing for either/both parties.

8.2   **Both parties agree and understand that all debts and liabilities set forth herein, unless otherwise specifically identified, are not "in the form of" or "in lieu of" maintenance or child support and therefore are specifically acknowledged as being dischargeable in bankruptcy.**

Article 8: Bankruptcy

Although referenced frequently in this book, bankruptcy issues are typically an all-or-nothing proposition when drafting the MSA. Either the clients are likely candidates, or they are not. Often, parties who are on the cusp of a bankruptcy make this a central issue in the negotiations. To avoid difficulties in arriving at an equitable distribution in the agreement and to aid in finalizing the MSA, it is often advisable to treat bankruptcy as strictly an "in the alternative" proposition. All other issues can then be resolved with the understanding that bankruptcy is only *an* option.

Additionally, by adding the above paragraph and bankruptcy language, both parties are alerted to the possibility of a future bankruptcy and how it may affect each in the division of debts and the ultimate liability thereon. Lately, it seems there has been a marked increase in clients returning to seek remedy in family court when a former spouse has availed himself or herself of bankruptcy protection. Unfortunately, such a reckoning is usually unattainable in family court, and the bankruptcy will likely discharge all of the former spouse's liability.

ARTICLE 9
FINANCIAL ACCOUNTS

9.1   **The Husband shall be awarded as his sole and exclusive property the proceeds of all financial accounts maintained in his name, except as otherwise set forth in this Marital Settlement Agreement.**

9.2   **The Wife shall be awarded as her sole and exclusive property the proceeds of all financial**

accounts maintained in her name, except as otherwise set forth in this Marital Settlement Agreement.

9.3   There are no joint accounts.

Article 9: Financial Accounts

Financial accounts can be addressed in various ways and in various areas of an MSA. By broad definition, financial accounts encompass both asset accounts and debt accounts. If all accounts in the form of indebtedness are accounted for in the various debt sections elsewhere in the MSA, then there is little likelihood of confusion. Therefore, by default, this section should concern only those accounts that are positive assets where title and ownership are easily modifiable, such as bank accounts, certificates of deposit, savings bonds, and investment accounts.

If possible, the parties should divide the asset accounts prior to the final draft of the MSA and the entry of the divorce. By dividing the accounts, the parties may be protected from adverse tax consequences or delays caused by the entry of the dissolution. Additionally, the parties are protected from any unexpected (and inappropriate) withdrawals between entry of the dissolution order and the anticipated distribution by either of the parties. Again, simple language is all that is needed if the accounts have been previously divided.

If the parties are unable to transfer appropriate funds to accommodate a simple division, additional specifics should set forth both how and when a transfer of funds shall take place. Such problematic divisions are typical in retirement, 401(k), and 403(b) accounts. These issues are dealt with in Section 10.0 below.

ARTICLE 10
PENSION AND RETIREMENT PLANS

10.1   The Husband shall be awarded all his pension and retirement benefits, vested and contingent, and all such future retirement accounts

**free of any claim of the Wife. The Husband waives
all rights to Wife's pension and retirement benefits,
vested, contingent and future.**

**10.2   The Wife shall be awarded all her pension and
retirement benefits, vested and contingent, and all
such future retirement accounts free of any claim of
the Husband. The Wife waives all rights to
Husband's pension and retirement benefits, vested,
contingent and future.**

**10.3   Both parties shall sign any necessary releases
of rights to benefits of said plans upon the entry of the
dissolution of marriage.**

Article 10: Pension and Retirement Plans

Retirement plans, or lack thereof, need to be addressed, as well. Even if the
parties represent that they have no retirement or pension, such plans may
still exist, but are not yet vested. This gives rise to the idea that such
retirements do not "exist." Likewise, if a party is in the military, his or her
retirement is not typically available until the twentieth year of service.
However, this does not mean there is not a marital percentage that may be
subject to division. To forestall any future claims to these non-vested
accounts or eliminate any confusion as to the existence of marital portions
that will later come to fruition, it is advisable to specifically dispose of the
accounts. Likewise, if the parties are correct and no retirement accounts
exist, language granting the ownership of the non-existent plans prevents
later contest.

In the example above, each party is awarded *all* his or her pension and
retirement accounts, real or anticipated.

General Marital Division

If the marital estate includes sufficient retirement assets to distribute among
the parties, or it is otherwise necessary to divide such assets, sufficient or
not, such a division is made typically in one of two ways. The first option is

to divide the asset pursuant to a set formula that protects both parties so that the participant in the plan is not penalized for continued service and growth of the retirement plan, and the non-participant's portion is not unreasonably reduced by such continuation and growth of said plan.

The second option is to divide an account with a finite dollar amount as of the date of the dissolution of marriage. The language below sets forth an example wherein both a dollar-specific account, such as a 401(k), is divided immediately, and an ongoing retirement plan is divided pursuant to the long-term formula approach regarding the husband's accounts. Any accounts not specifically awarded are to remain the sole and exclusive property of the husband. Additionally, in this example, the wife retains her accounts, as in the previous example.

ALTERNATIVE PROVISION – GENERAL MARITAL DIVISION

10.1   The Husband shall be awarded all his pension and retirement benefits, vested and contingent, and all such future retirement accounts free of any claim of the Wife except to the extent set forth below regarding his A.G. Edwards 401k and his Pipe Fitters Union retirement account. The Husband waives all rights to Wife's pension and retirement benefits, vested, contingent and future.

10.2   The Wife shall be awarded all her pension and retirement benefits, vested and contingent, and all such future retirement accounts free of any claim of the Husband. The Wife waives all rights to Husband's pension and retirement benefits, vested, contingent and future except her marital portion of his A.G. Edwards 401k and his Pipe Fitters Union retirement account set forth in paragraphs 10.3 and 10.4 below.

10.3   The Wife shall be awarded 80% of the Husband's A.G. Edwards 401k account as valued on the date of the dissolution of marriage. Said division is an offset to the Wife's marital equity in the marital home awarded to the husband in Section 2 above. It is mutually understood that there has been no withdrawals or loans on said account as of the date of this instrument by either party. Additionally, neither party shall take any action with regard to the 401k account until the entry of the Dissolution of Marriage. The parties shall cooperate in the transfer of said funds. The Wife shall be responsible for the preparation and entry of any forms, Qualified Domestic Relations Orders or any other documentation necessary for the transfer. The transfer shall be completed within six (6) months of the entry of the Dissolution of Marriage Order. The Wife shall be responsible for any cost associated with the transfer including any tax consequences if the funds are withdrawn and not placed with another qualified tax exempt account.

In the example of 10.3, a disproportionate share of the account was awarded to the wife to offset equity of another marital asset. Such description is not necessary, but is an effective tool in this section, as well as other sections throughout the agreement, to explain any deviation from an essentially equal division of assets.

10.4   The Wife shall also be awarded her marital portion of the Husband's retirement plan with the Pipe Fitters Union which shall be divided as follows:

$$\frac{\textit{Number of months married while the husband was in the plan}}{\textit{Total number of months in the plan}} \times \textit{½} = \begin{array}{l}\textit{wife's portion of}\\ \textit{the retirement benefit}\end{array}$$

Said formula setting forth the total number of months the parties were married while the Husband was active in the plan as the numerator and the total number of months the Husband is in the plan as the denominator, multiplied by ½ (the marital share) thus equaling the Wife's marital portion of the Husband's retirement benefit. Said benefit to be paid pursuant to the underlying retirement plan and set forth in a Qualified Domestic Relations Order to be executed by both parties and entered herewith. The Wife shall have the QDRO prepared and entered at her expense within six (6) months of the entry of the Dissolution of Marriage Order.

10.5   Both parties to sign and execute all necessary documentation and aforesaid QDROs to effect said transfers within seven (7) days of presentation to the other party.

<u>Military Retirement</u>

For any practice located in close proximity to a military base, military divorces are likely a large percentage your case load. Of course, with the mobility of society today, it is likely you will encounter a military divorce at some time in your practice. The example below sets forth a static division of the husband's thrift savings plan (TSP), which is substantially similar to a 401(k) account, and the additional language necessary to divide the military retirement account.

Of particular note is the 20-10 rule. This is the common understanding that a serviceperson needs to have twenty years of creditable service (service that qualifies toward his or her retirement), and the spouse must have been married to the serviceperson for ten of those years to qualify for his or her marital share. Thus, a marriage of only eight or nine years may deny the spouse any retirement benefit pursuant to military rule. However, this is not necessarily the only option. In Illinois, the court exercises jurisdiction over the parties, not the military. So in certain circumstances, the court may award a percentage of any retirement (military or otherwise) to be paid by the recipient to the ex-spouse upon his or her receipt of the actual funds. This direct-pay option can be utilized either in the maintenance portion of the MSA or by artfully modifying the example above. Particular care should be exercised in drafting such terms. Because of the unique and fact-based situations wherein these options arise, an example is not being provided herein.

Assuming a marriage that otherwise qualifies for a military division of assets is at hand, the following example is appropriate for such a division.

ALTERNATIVE PROVISION – MILITARY

10.1   The Husband shall be awarded all his pension and retirement benefits, vested and contingent, and all such future retirement accounts free of any claim of the Wife except to the extent set forth below regarding his Thrift Savings Plan and his Military Retirement. The Husband waives all rights to Wife's pension and retirement benefits, vested, contingent and future.

10.2   The Wife shall be awarded all her pension and retirement benefits, vested and contingent, and all such future retirement accounts free of any claim of the Husband. The Wife waives all rights to Husband's pension and retirement benefits, vested, contingent and future except her marital portion of his Thrift Savings Plan and his Military Retirement as set forth in the remaining paragraphs of this section.

10.3   The Wife shall be awarded $25,000.00 (twenty five thousand dollars) as her portion of the Husband's Thrift Savings Plan (TSP) account. Additionally, neither party shall take any action with regard to the TSP account until the entry of the Dissolution of Marriage. The parties shall cooperate in the transfer of said funds. The Wife shall be responsible for the preparation and entry of any forms, Qualified Domestic Relations Orders or any other documentation necessary for the transfer. The transfer shall be completed within six (6) months of the entry of the Dissolution of Marriage Order. The Wife shall be responsible for any cost associated with the transfer including any tax consequences if the funds

*are withdrawn and not placed with another qualified
tax exempt account.*

*10.4 The Wife shall be awarded a monthly
percentage share of Husband's United States Air
Force retainer/retired pay upon Husband's
retirement from the United States Air Force. Said
award shall be in accordance with and construed by
the Uniformed Services Former Spouses' Protection
Act of September 8, 1982 (public law 97-252). Wife's
monthly percentage share shall be determined by the
following formula:*

$$\frac{\text{Number of months married while the husband was in the service while obtaining creditable time}}{\text{Total number of months the Husband is/was in the service obtaining creditable time.}} \quad X \quad \tfrac{1}{2} \quad = \quad \text{Wife's portion of the retirement benefit}$$

*Disposable military retired/retainer pay as used
herein means Husband's gross military
retired/retainer pay less only those amounts properly
withheld for Federal, State and local income taxes.
The share of the disposable military retired/retainer
pay shall commence upon the Husband's receipt of
the retired/retainer pay and shall continue until the
death of either party. OR The Husband and Wife
shall select the Surviving Spouse Benefit Plan (SBP)
and the Wife shall be identified as the recipient of the
SBP benefit. The cost of the SBP shall be deducted
from the Husband's OR Wife's portion of his OR her
retirement benefit. The Wife will OR will not be
entitled to Cost Of Living Allowances (COLA).*

Additional issues of the surviving spouse benefit and the cost of living
allowance should be addressed by either allowing the benefit and allocating
the cost thereof or specifically denying the benefit.

10.5   Under the terms of the Uniformed Services Former Spouses' Protection Act, the United States Air Force as the paying authority is required to directly pay Wife her monthly percentage share of Husband's monthly disposable military retired/retainer pay because of the following: In the course of the parties' marriage, Husband performed at least ten (10) years of service creditable in determining his eligibility for retired/retainer pay. The parties were married on April 1, 1998, and divorced on (enter date of entry of Dissolution)   , 201__. Husband began service creditable in determining his eligibility for retired/retainer pay with the United States Air Force on (enter date Husband began creditable service   , has performed continuous creditable service since then and is now on active duty with the United States Air Force. Husband's full name and social security number are: Richard Smith, XXX-XX-1234. Wife's full name and social security number are: Rose Smith, XXX-XX-4321.

Most courts have now enacted redaction rules barring the inclusion of full Social Security numbers. For military purposes, it is advisable to have a redacted and full copy signed and entered, with the full copy being sent to the military. Alternatively, you may have only redacted copies entered and then send the additional information via cover letter or other military document, such as the DD2293, which is used in conjunction with the marital settlement agreement retirement section.

10.6   The court finds that the Husband' military retired/retainer pay is and shall be accruing as a result of his service in the United States Air Force and that the military retired/retainer pay is marital property subject to equitable division by the family court of the Circuit Court of St. Clair County, Illinois, pursuant to Illinois Statutes. The court further finds that it is competent to divide the parties' marital property incident to their divorce pursuant to Illinois law. The court finally finds that it has jurisdiction over the Husband for the purpose of dividing his disposable military retired/retainer pay because the Husband has consented to the court's jurisdiction to divide his disposable military are retired/retainer pay.

10.7   Husband has been afforded his rights under the Soldiers' and Sailors Civil Relief Act of 1940 (50 U.S.C. Appendix 501-591).

10.8   The court shall retain jurisdiction over Husband's military retired/retainer pay for so long as the parties both shall live. The court shall also have the authority to make every just and equitable order not inconsistent with the other provisions herein, and not inconsistent with the Uniformed Services Former Spouses' Protection Act or any other applicable law. The court shall also have specific authority to make any orders it deems just and equitable as a result of the income tax consequences which flow from the division and distribution of the retired/retainer pay.

10.9   The court shall also have continuing jurisdiction to make every order reasonably necessary to implement and accomplish the direct payment to Wife by the United States Air Force of her percentage share of Husband's disposable military retired/retainer pay, including the right to advise the United States Air Force of the precise amount or percentage of Husband's disposable military retired/retainer pay to be payable to Wife.

ARTICLE 11
PERSONAL INJURY CLAIMS / LAWSUITS

11.1   The Husband has a personal injury claim now pending in the State of Illinois against Metro Transit Authority. The settlement or award shall be divided such that the Husband shall be awarded 75% of the proceeds after all outstanding liens, costs, expenses of litigation and attorney fees are assessed. The Wife shall be awarded 25% of any settlement or award after all outstanding liens, costs, expenses of litigation and attorney fees are assessed.

11.2 The Wife has a loss of consortium claim pending as part of the Husband's claim now pending against the Metro Transit Authority. The settlement or award shall be divided such that the Wife shall be awarded 75% of the proceeds after all outstanding liens, costs, expenses of litigation and attorney fees are assessed. The Husband shall be awarded 25% of any settlement or award after all outstanding liens, costs, expenses of litigation and attorney fees are assessed.

Article 11: Personal Injury Claims/Lawsuits

On occasion, one or both parties may have pending lawsuits at the time of the dissolution process. Typically, any injury or cause of action that came into being during the marriage is deemed a marital asset and should be accounted for as such. Consideration should be given to the extent of the injuries, the future income potential, and even such additional causes of action as loss of consortium. Additionally, each claim or individual cause of action should be addressed. Finally, language that addresses issues of costs, liens, and sometimes tax consequences should be set forth.

ARTICLE 12
BUSINESS INTERESTS

12.1 The Husband shall be awarded all interest and stock in the Corporation known as "Smith Carpentry, Inc." as incorporated in the State of Illinois as his sole and exclusive property. The Husband shall be awarded the Corporation and all its assets and inventory, including but not limited to, a

Ford F250 pickup truck, all tools and equipment necessary for the ordinary course of business, and the bank accounts held in the corporation's name at Regions Bank.

12. 2 The Wife shall sign and transfer all stock certificates held by her to the Husband within 30 days of the entry of the Dissolution of Marriage and relinquish her position as Vice President via letter of resignation addressed to all shareholders.

Article 12: Business Interests

Just as with the marital home discussed earlier in the real estate section, a business owned by one or both parties can be one of the most valuable assets of a marriage. Actual value and the sweat equity in such enterprises may not always be ascertainable. Relative values can be offset via awards of various other marital property items, retirements, and equity in other investments. Such division need only be set forth in those respective sections. However the business is divided, through stock ownership, partnership transfers, or an entire award of the entity, the full terms need to be set forth.

In the example above, the business is being awarded solely to the husband, inclusive of a business vehicle (not otherwise accounted for in the vehicle section above because its title is being held by the corporation), the inventory, bank accounts, and tools of the trade. If the assets of the corporation appear to be intermingled with the marital assets, a full accounting of such items should be included or otherwise made identifiable for enforcement purposes.

Child-Related Matters

If the parties have children, the following sections apply to the financial aspects of the divorce regarding the children.

ARTICLE 13
PARENTING AGREEMENT

13.1   The parties have voluntarily entered into a Parenting Agreement regarding the custody and visitation of their child(ren) which is to be made part of this Marital Settlement Agreement and entered as part of the final Dissolution of Marriage Order. The parties each believe said Parenting Agreement is fair, equitable and in the best interest of the minor child(ren).

Article 13: Parenting Agreement

Often, attorneys combine all agreed issues, including the terms and conditions of the parenting agreement, into the marital settlement agreement. Although this is a viable option, I prefer to separate the agreements into two documents that are subsequently enrolled into the final order. Many times a school or other entity will require a copy of the parenting agreement, and there is little need to share the extraneous and often personal financial information contained in a party's MSA.

However, referencing the parenting agreement and acknowledging the "fair and equitable" nature of the parenting agreement in the MSA (as set forth above) allays any fear and confronts specifically any claim that the terms or conditions of the MSA have been an inducement into, or have been predicated on, the acceptance of the terms of the parenting agreement.

ARTICLE 14
CHILD SUPPORT

14.1   The Husband agrees that he will pay to the Wife, the sum of $800.00 per month beginning on the first day of _____, 201___ and continuing on or before the first (1st) day of each month thereafter as child support until such time as the children have attained the age of nineteen (19) or graduated from high school, whichever comes first. The parties affirm

that said amount is a deviation from the statutory guideline of 32% of the Husband's statutory net income. Said deviation is due to the time each parent will share with the children and the respective incomes of each party. Additionally, the parties acknowledge that child support is always modifiable and may be adjusted upon request of either party. Any modification shall be made by the court taking into account all applicable statutory provisions.

Article 14: Child Support

Child support amounts are typically defined by statute and are typically a set percentage of net income or a comprehensive calculation based on the income and needs of each parent and the needs of the child. However, parties often supersede statutory authority when negotiating a resolution to their pending divorce. Provided there is adequate reason, and those reasons are clearly set forth, deviation from the statutory guidelines is generally accepted by the court. Additionally, child support is for the benefit of the minor children and may be modifiable as income of the parties changes and the needs of the children increase. In the example above, the child support is acknowledged as such a deviation, with the caveat that either party may petition the court for future modification.

Child support is usually intended to cover the payer's portion of the routine expenses incurred by the custodial parent for the children, such as clothing, activity fees, and school fees. However, if the children attend private school or have other cost-intensive activities, additional language can be added to cover these expenses or, alternatively, be provided as good cause for the court to deviate from the statutory guidelines.

ADDITIONAL PROVISION

Additionally, the husband shall each pay ½ (one-half) of the Private School tuition for the years Kindergarten through 12th grade and ½ (one-half) of the necessary educational expenses incurred by the children until graduation from High School. The Wife

> *will pay the fees initially and submit the receipts to the Husband within 10 days. The Husband will reimburse the Wife within 21 days. The Husband will also pay ½ (one-half) of the children's extra circular fees for each child at the beginning of each season/ activity fee period.*

Clients should be advised that specific expenses, ostensibly in lieu of child support, might not be modifiable. As such, a party should be cautious in selecting this option. Unforeseen financial circumstances may arise, creating a devastating financial effect and subjecting the non-paying parent to contempt proceedings on a liability he or she cannot modify.

In Illinois, the State Disbursement Unit (SDU) now handles child support payments. Most local court rules further require that all payments be made through this service. A withholding order is sent to the payer's employer, who is then statutorily required to comply. When payments are made through the SDU, there is the assumption that a comprehensive record will be maintained of payment and compliance.

> **14.2   Payments shall be made by Order of Withholding through the State Disbursement Unit. The Wife shall prepare a withholding order and serve same upon the Husband's employer within 7 days of the entry of Dissolution of Marriage. The Husband shall apprize the Wife of any change in employment within 14 days of said change and provide all necessary contact information for his employer.**

Alternatively, if the spouse is self-employed or it is otherwise advisable to self-pay, provisions can be incorporated that must be approved by the court. Additionally, language requiring payment through the SDU if the payer spouse fails is recommended. In all circumstances, payment via cash is not advised. There is simply no way to track cash payments.

ALTERNATIVE PROVISION

14.2   Payments of child support shall be made directly to the Wife by the Husband by Check or Money Order. In the event that the Husband obtains alternate employment or otherwise becomes more than thirty (30) days late in his child support obligation, the Wife may immediately serve his employer or the Husband individually a withholding order requiring all future payments be made through the State Disbursement Unit.

Finally, the parties' ability to claim the minor children on subsequent tax filings should be addressed as part of the child support negotiations. Pursuant to federal law, the individual claiming a child must supply at least one-half of the child's expenses yearly. This, however, is likely at issue only if one spouse later challenges the exemption claimed directly with the Internal Revenue Service (IRS). The state court, based on personal jurisdiction, and the parties through negotiation, can balance the right to the children's exemptions with that of child support paid.

In most cases, if child support is minimal, one would default to the argument that federal law should ultimately control, thereby vesting the custodial parent with the yearly deduction. In the alternative, if child support is arguably sufficient to meet the constraints of the federal regulations, exemptions can be split based on the totality of the parties' negotiations.

ADDITIONAL PROVISIONS

14.3   The Wife shall claim the minor child, Gwen Smith, on all subsequent tax filings made to the Federal and State Government until it is no longer economically feasible.

14.4   The Husband shall claim the minor child, George Smith, on all subsequent tax filings made to the Federal and State Government until it is no longer economically feasible.

14.5   The parties shall alternate claiming the minor child, Sidney Smith, on subsequent tax filings made to the Federal and State Government, such that the Wife claims the minor child for even numbered years beginning the tax year 2010 (as to be filed April 15, 2011) and the Husband shall claim the minor child for odd numbered years beginning the tax year 2011 (as to be filed April 15, 2012). The parties shall continue alternating claiming said child until it is no longer economically feasible.

14.6   Both parties shall sign any necessary documents and submit same to the Internal Revenue Service to allow the parties to claim the minor children subject the division set forth above.

ARTICLE 15
HEALTH INSURANCE/MEDICAL BILLS

15.1   The Husband shall maintain health insurance for the benefit of the minor child. He shall furnish the Wife with an insurance card and update her timely of any benefit changes or change in providers.

Article 15: Health Insurance and Uncovered Medical Expense

Closely associated with, if not inseparable from, child support is the issue of health insurance. Just as child support is for the benefit of the child for necessities such as housing, food, clothing, and education, health insurance is necessary for the well-being of the child. Although state-sponsored programs are usually available for the fiscally challenged, placing the burden of providing health insurance on one or both of the parents is advisable to ensure the best possible care for the children and does not unreasonably burden the parent least able to provide such insurance.

Historically, husbands have been the least likely to be granted custody and the most likely to pay child support. They have also been the most likely to have health insurance as a benefit of employment. So the burden of supplying health insurance for the minor children has fallen on husbands.

Times have changed, but there is still the assumption that the payer spouse, or "obligor spouse" as to child support, is that party who also remains liable for the payment of health insurance benefits. Despite this presupposition, either party may be required to pay for the insurance on the minor children.

When considering child support obligations, the cost of health insurance should be factored in to the equation. Additionally, much weight should be given to the quality of the insurance and the stability of the obligor spouse's employment when assigning responsibility for maintaining such policies.

The example above sets forth simple language wherein the husband shall remain responsible for the children's health care insurance, dental, optical, and so on.

Additional provisions should be included to encompass those expenses not covered by insurance. Both co-pay expenses and deductible issues are best resolved with time-specific language.

> **15.2   The Wife shall pay any uncovered expenses (co-pay expenses) at the time of treatment and shall furnish proof of payment to the Husband within 30 days of such treatment. The Husband shall reimburse the Wife one-half (1/2) of said expense within 14 days.**

> **15.3   Any medical, dental, optical, psychiatric, orthodontic or prescription expenses incurred on behalf of the child not covered by insurance (after all insurance payments have been applied) shall be divided equally by the parties directly to the provider within 30 days unless a payment schedule is arranged through said provider.**

Finally, that the parties are resolving the matters at hand does not mean games cannot be played later. Unfortunately, children (or issues revolving around the children) seem to be a preferred avenue to extract vengeance on the other party. To prevent a parent from choosing providers outside a network to increase costs to the other parent, it can be worthwhile to include language sufficient to shift the financial burden to the parent seeking such care.

ADDITIONAL PROVISION

> ***15.4   If either party intentionally (excluding emergency treatment) seeks treatment for the children outside the policy providers under the Husband's insurance plan, that party shall be solely responsible for uncovered costs.***

ARTICLE 16
COLLEGE EXPENSES

The parties agree that the issues of college expenses for the minor children are hereby reserved.

Article 16: College Expense

College expense or non-minor expense is a category that is often better left to negotiation or hearing later. The scholastic aptitude of the child or children may not be known during the divorce. Additionally, other contingencies, such as scholarships and even the ultimate preferences of the children, will factor heavily into the college or trade school a child may attend. Therefore, if the children are young, a reservation of the issue may be the best option.

Practice note: The courts in Illinois have affirmed that a reservation of the college expenses is not a bar to determining that the dissolution of marriage order is a final and appealable order and has no detrimental effect to appeal, enforcement, or modification of custody petitions. You should verify the statutory and case law for the jurisdiction in which you practice.

However, if a determination is necessary due to jurisdiction, or the children are otherwise of an age to warrant a settlement on the issue of college expense, an example is supplied below.

When dividing the respective responsibility of the non-minor expenses, custody is no longer at issue. The child is, essentially, an emancipated adult. Therefore, either or both parties may be responsible for these expenses. The adult child plays a vital role in this matter, as well. His or her choice of schools, eligibility for scholarships and grants, and ability to work and contribute to his or her education may greatly affect the proceedings.

Now, more than ever, the income and expenses of both parents should factor into their ability to pay. Therefore, committing a party (or both parties) to a specific division is a decision worthy of serious consideration.

ALTERNATIVE PROVISIONS –
SPECIFIC DIVISION

16.1   The Husband agrees that he will pay 50% of the vocational school, college or university education for the child(ren) of the parties, which obligation is predicated upon the scholastic aptitude of each child.

16.2   The Wife agrees that she will pay 25% for the vocational school, college or university education for the child(ren) of the parties, which obligation is predicated upon the scholastic aptitude of each child.

Although not necessary, many parents choose to make the child pay some of his or her own expenses to ensure a vested interest in the education.

OPTIONAL PROVISIONS

16.3   The child attending such vocational school, college or university shall be responsible for the remaining 25% of the costs of his or her education.

The parties need to further understand that the child seeking higher education is likely a legal adult. Therefore, consideration must be provided to the child as to his or her wishes. Ultimately, it may not be the parties' decision, but a decision made by the court to alleviate any stalemate. So the following language should be incorporated.

16.4   Decisions affecting the post secondary education of the children, including the choice of the school to be attended, shall be made jointly by the parties and shall consider the expressed preference of the child. Neither party shall unreasonably withhold his or her consent to the expressed preference of the child. In the event the parties are unable to agree upon the school to be attended or upon any of the foregoing, then a court of competent jurisdiction shall make the determination upon proper notice and petition.

The parties obligated themselves to a percentage in Paragraphs 16.1 and 16.2, but what did they obligate themselves to? A relatively comprehensive list is included in the example below. However, items such as transportation and activity fees may be better left to the student or otherwise redistributed into his or her responsibility or share of the expenses in Paragraph 16.3 above.

16.5   The parties agree that college expenses shall be defined as all the costs and expenses necessarily incurred while pursuing said education, including but not limited to, college application fees, tuition, room and board, books, laboratory and activity fees, clothing, transportation expenses, student health fees, and any other expense usually or ordinarily incurred in the acquisition of a vocational school, college or university education for a period of up to 5 years of attendance at said school(s).

With the division of responsibility established, it may still be necessary to obtain student loans, parent/student loans, or even second mortgages to manage the costs associated with these expenses. Parties may utilize these options in a 50/25/25 split (as previously set forth in Sections 16.1, 16.2, and 16.3, above) as they go along, or they may consolidate all costs and loans associated therewith and arrange payments according to the ratio of responsibility. In any event, the parties should understand that such an agreement as to responsibility of payment will survive graduation and continue until such loans are paid in full.

> *16.6   Any expenses in the form of student loans or other deferred payment arrangements shall be maintained and paid in the ratio set forth in paragraphs 16.1, 16.2 and 16.3 above as to the entirety of the costs incurred.*

Additionally, termination of responsibility should be included. If the student fails to perform adequately, is on a   six-year-plus program, is academically or behaviorally removed from the curriculum, or otherwise ceases in his or her pursuit of higher education, the parents need to be absolved of their continuing duty of assistance.

> *16.7   The Husband's and Wife's obligation to continue payment except those already incurred as set forth in paragraph 16.6 shall immediately terminate in the event that the child fails to maintain at least a C average (3.0 on a 4.0 scale) for more than two semesters, ceases to matriculate (for any reason) at such a vocational, college or university for more than one semester, or by written agreement of the parties.*

The example provided that both parties and the child were subject to payment of expenses. If the situation warrants, any combination of the above can be considered.

ARTICLE 17
INCOME TAXES

17.1   The Husband, Richard Smith, affirmatively states that he has paid his portion of all income taxes, state and federal, on all returns filed by the parties (jointly or separately) during the course of their marriage. The Husband further acknowledges that if additional liability is assessed as a result of the joint or separate tax returns filed by the parties (or

amendments thereto), as filed during the course of the marriage, he shall fully indemnify and hold harmless the Wife for any liability, tax deficiency, penalty or interest, together with any costs expended in the defense of any claimed tax deficiency resulting from the filing of said tax returns, by reason of any information set forth on said return which is attributable to his income or his deductions based on information furnished by him on said returns. In the event additional refunds or stimulus payments are paid or received as ≈ result of any tax returns filed while the parties were married, said funds shall be divided pro-rata based on the respective incomes of the parties at the time the return was processed.

17.2   The Wife, Rose Smith, affirmatively states that she has paid her portion of all income taxes, state and federal, on all returns filed by the parties (jointly or separately) during the course of their marriage. The Wife further acknowledges that if additional liability is assessed as a result of the joint or separate tax returns filed by the parties (or amendments thereto), as filed during the course of the marriage, she shall fully indemnify and hold harmless the Husband for any liability, tax deficiency, penalty or interest, together with any costs expended in the defense of any claimed tax deficiency resulting from the filing of said tax returns, by reason of any information set forth on said return which is attributable to her income or her deductions based on information furnished by her on said returns. In the event additional refunds or stimulus payments are paid or received as a result of any tax returns filed while the parties were married, said funds shall be divided pro-rata based on the respective incomes of the parties at the time the return was processed.

17.3 The parties agree and acknowledge that if additional liability is assessed as a result of the joint or separate tax returns filed by the parties (or amendments thereto), during the course of the marriage, as a result of mutual mistake, the parties shall share said liability (including the costs expended in the defense of any claimed tax deficiency) pro-rata based on the respective incomes of the parties at the time the return was processed.

17.4 The parties agree that if it becomes necessary to file amendments to any returns for the years in which the parties where married, they will fully cooperate with each other and the requesting entity, including providing necessary documentation, and authorizing third parties to represent each of them in connection with preparing amended returns or any related issue to said tax filings. The parties shall provide each other with copies of any amended returns as filed.

Article 17: Income Tax

In life, there is the certainty of taxes. In divorce, there is the certainty of taxes. Neither party should therefore trust in candid disclosure by the other spouse when it comes to the parties' tax filings. This section on income taxes attempts to encompass all taxing authorities and the respective liabilities of each party, past, present, and future.

In Paragraphs 17.1 and 17.2 above, each party assumes liability for all his or her "mistakes" that may have been made in the filing of the parties' marital tax returns. While unusual for parties to have to avail themselves of the protection of these paragraphs, catastrophic results may be avoided by including the language set forth in the example below.

Additionally, any "fortuitous mistakes" resulting in a refund or return are addressed and awarded pro-rata based on the parties' income at the time of filing. Alternatively, these funds can be divided equally or in any other manner the parties find to be equitable. Finally, the possibility of a mutual mistake resulting in joint liability is addressed in Paragraph 17.3. Financial responsibility is then divided pro-rata.

Paragraph 17.4 should be included to ensure cooperation between the parties if any amendments or other action becomes necessary.

The past and future issues being ostensibly resolved above, the practitioners need look to present tax issues. Since transfers between spouses are almost unilaterally non-taxable events, an uncontested or negotiated divorce can resolve many potential tax issues by accomplishing the transfers discussed throughout this book contemporaneously with the finalizing of the MSA, but prior to the entry of the dissolution of marriage order. However, other assets, such as retirement accounts, must await the final order and documentation, including, but not limited to, qualified domestic relations orders. Whether transfers are complete before or after the entry of the dissolution, the parties should be advised of potential tax consequences. The language in Paragraphs 17.5 and 17.6 do not set forth all such potential consequences, but alerts the client of his or her responsibilities.

> **17.5   The parties agree that the division and transfers of property made pursuant to this Agreement are incident to the divorce of the parties. No gain or loss (capital or otherwise) shall be claimed in connection with the transfer of property or money provided by this Agreement except as to any taxable transfers from qualified retirement plans. The tax basis attributable to all property affected by this Agreement shall remain the tax basis which the property had prior to the dissolution of marriage. The party receiving any property hereunder shall be responsible for any tax liability associated therewith and shall hold the other party harmless from any and all such tax liability including interest and penalties.**

17. 6   **The parties understand that each must file a separate individual tax return in the forthcoming tax year and that all claims and deductions shall be made consistent with the terms and conditions set forth above.**

ARTICLE 18
ATTORNEY'S FEES

18.1   **Each party shall pay all of his or her own attorneys' fees and costs incurred in these proceedings and shall indemnify and hold the other harmless with respect thereto.**

Article 18: Attorney's Fees

Although either party could be ordered to pay the other's attorney fees, seldom is a party willing to volunteer. Thus, any division of attorney fees can be the "deal breaker" and as such, the most common settlement between parties is for each to pay his or her own attorney fees.

It is often advisable to maintain the appearance of an equal split of these particular "debts," notwithstanding the likelihood that other assets that have been split will, in essence, pay these fees.

However, if a party is willing to pay a portion of the other party's fees, specific language should be included to set forth a specific dollar amount. It is also advisable to have your client pay you and thereafter be reimbursed directly by the other spouse. This avoids the necessity of collection activity by the law firm against the other party.

ALTERNATIVE PROVISION

18.1   The Husband shall pay all of his attorney fees and hold harmless the Wife with respect thereto. The Husband shall also reimburse the Wife the sum of $3,000.00 as and for a portion of her attorney fees incurred herein. The Husband shall pay said sum *directly to the Wife within 60 (sixty) days of the entry of Dissolution of Marriage.*

Finally, it is advisable to notify the parties of their right to a hearing (in Illinois) on the division of fees, despite their agreement herein.

18.2   Husband and Wife acknowledge that they are fully advised of their right to a full and complete hearing as to their attorneys' fees and costs under the Illinois Marriage and Dissolution of Marriage Act (750 ILCS 5/508), and the right to request the other party's contribution to her of his or her attorney's fees and costs under said Act (750 ILCS 5/503(j)), and have knowingly and voluntarily waived their right to a contribution hearing.

<u>ARTICLE 19</u>
<u>GENERAL PROVISIONS</u>

19.1   <u>Execution of Documents:</u> Each party shall agree to execute and deliver, concurrently with the execution hereof, all documents or instruments necessary to vest the titles and estates in the respective parties hereto as sole and separate ownership and to otherwise carry out the purposes of this Agreement. If either party shall fail or refuse to execute any such documents, then this Agreement shall constitute a full and present transfer, assignment and conveyance of all rights hereinabove designated to be transferred, assigned and conveyed, and a full, present and effective relinquishment and wavier of all rights hereinabove designated to be relinquished and waived. If either party fails for a period of more than 30 days after the effective date of this agreement to make, execute acknowledge or deliver any necessary documents or instruments which are reasonably required to implement the terms of this agreement, a judicial officer of the Circuit Court for the Twentieth

Judicial Circuit, St. Clair County, Illinois is hereby authorized to make, execute acknowledge, and deliver such documents and instruments at the request of either party. This authorization includes, but shall not be limited to, any and all documents and instruments pertaining to the transfer or conveyance of real and personal property and beneficiary interests in land trusts.

Article 19: General Provisions

The MSA is ultimately a contract, which is then submitted to a court for approval and made an order of the court via incorporation. No contract would be complete without the general provisions that serve to tie up any remaining issues and create enforceability in the event of a breach, material or otherwise.

Paragraph 19.1 above requires completion of any necessary paperwork within a specific time and provides the court specific authority to either enforce the completion or, in the alternative, sign in the place of the breaching party to effect all transfers agreed to within the marital settlement agreement.

19.2 Mutual Releases: To the fullest extent permitted by law, and except as otherwise provided herein, each of the parties does hereby forever release, waive and quitclaim all rights of maintenance, alimony, inheritance, descent and distribution, homestead, dower, community interest and all other interest and estate as husband and wife, widow or widower, including any and all right, title, claim or interest which he or she might have or be entitled to claim in, to or against the property, assets and estate of the other, whether real, personal or marital or non-marital, whether community or separate, whether now owned or hereafter in any manner acquired by the other party, whether in possession or in expectancy and whether vested or contingent.

Paragraph 19.2 accounts for the release of all claims not otherwise specifically set forth in the previous portion of the MSA. It should be noted there is a waiver of maintenance, formerly known as alimony, after the language "except as otherwise provided herein." The references to maintenance or alimony should be eliminated if the prior maintenance provisions awarded *permanent* maintenance to avoid confusion. Otherwise, the mutual releases serve to sever any other claims the parties may have, now and in the future.

As with any contract, the construction of the agreement should not serve to obscure the terms and meaning of the agreement, but to define it.

19.3 <u>Construction of Agreement</u>:

    A. The recitals set forth at the commencement of this Agreement are intended to be and are made a part of this Agreement.

    B. The captions contained in this Agreement are for convenience only and are not intended to limit or define the scope or effect of any provision of this Agreement.

    C. Any word in the text of this Agreement shall be read as singular or as plural and as masculine, feminine or neuter gender as may be appropriate under the circumstances to carry out the parties' intent.

A divorce is meant to be a final resolution between the parties. No portion should be modifiable unless specifically set forth or in regard to any *minor* children of the marriage. The parties should understand that the negotiations will not continue after entry with the court, and the MSA will be an enforceable part of the court's final order.

    D. The provisions of this Agreement except as specifically set forth herein and as to, custody, support or visitation of the child shall not be subject to subsequent modification by any

> **Court, except by mutual written consent of the parties or; except as otherwise set forth in specific sections above.**

In addition to this agreement becoming an order of court, it is also subject to being represented as a comprehensive settlement of all issues between the parties. If the parties have made an agreement, it should be set forth in this or another court document. As with contract law, outside promises are not enforceable, nor will they be sufficient to set aside a fully informed consent to entry of a final order.

> **E. The provisions of this Agreement contain the entire understanding of the parties. No representations, warranties, promises, covenants or undertakings other than those expressly set forth herein have been made by either party to the other.**

> **F. This Agreement shall be construed under the general laws of the State of Illinois, irrespective of the later domicile or residence of Husband and Wife.**

To protect the parties from a subsequent invalidation of any one portion of this agreement, this boilerplate language ensures the remaining document is enforceable.

> **G. It is expressly understood and agreed between the parties that in the event a court of competent jurisdiction at that time after the entry of a Judgment of Dissolution of Marriage holds that a portion of this Agreement is invalid or unenforceable, the remainder hereof shall not be affected thereby and shall continue in full force and effect.**

Finally, the parties indicate that upon entry of the dissolution of marriage, all terms and conditions set forth herein become effective, and thus enforceable.

> **H. This Agreement shall become effective in the event and upon the date a Judgment of Dissolution of Marriage is entered in this cause.**

The indemnity paragraph below is boilerplate language that is rarely, like most boilerplate language, negotiable. However, it defines the responsibility of each party concerning the debts and will likely be used by a court in the event enforcement is made necessary.

> **19.4   Indemnity: The term indemnity or indemnify as used in this Agreement shall mean that the party agreeing to indemnify (the "Indemnitor") agrees to secure and save the other party (the "Indemnitee") from potential or actual loss which includes: any and all of Indemnitee's attorneys' fees or other expenses incurred by the Indemnitee in investigating or defending against any claim or for enforcing the provisions of the indemnity.**

As stated earlier, attorney fees can be a "deal breaker" or, in Section 19.6 below, the "great equalizer." Parties should be advised that any substantive breach or breach requiring court intervention shall result in attorney fees to be paid by the breaching party pursuant to Section 19.6. Additionally, each party reserves the right to avail himself or herself of court intervention under the Illinois Marriage and Dissolution of Marriage Act in Section 19.7, below.

> **19.6   Enforcement: In the event either party requires intervention from the Court for enforcement of any provision herein, as a result of a breach or default by the other party, the breaching/defaulting party shall pay the reasonable attorney's fees and costs incurred by the other in connection with such enforcement action.**

> **19.7   Reservation of Rights: Each party reserves the right to prosecute or defend any action now pending or which may hereafter be brought for relief under the Illinois Marriage and Dissolution of Marriage Act.**

Article 20: Closing and Signatures

The entire purpose of entering into negotiations and ultimately resolving the pending issues is to fully and fairly settle all outstanding matters and obtain a dissolution of marriage. The statements below reiterate this consensus and request incorporation into the final order.

20.1   Each party agrees that his or her acceptance of the terms set forth in this Agreement represents a full and final settlement of any claims he or she may have in and to any of the property, either marital or non-marital, now owned or hereinafter acquired by his or her spouse, whether real, personal or inadvertently excluded. The parties agree that the distribution of property outlined in this Article is fair and equitable.

20.2   FURTHER, The parties agree that the terms of this Agreement shall be made the Order of this Court if this Agreement is approved by the Court.

Finally, it is advisable, if not necessary, to have each party's signature notarized because of the incorporated entry of appearance in Paragraph C in the Introduction section, above, as well as the financial division of assets.

Dated: _____   _____
Richard Smith

STATE OF ILLINOIS   )
**   )'**
COUNTY OF ST. CLAIR   )

I, _____, a Notary Public in and for said County in the State aforesaid, do hereby certify that _____, personally known to me to be the same person whose name is subscribed to the

within instrument of writing, appeared before me this day in person and acknowledged that he signed the same as his free and voluntary act, for the uses and purposes therein set forth.

Given under my hand and notarial seal this _____ day of _____, 201__.

_____

Notary Public

Dated: _____   _____

Rose Smith

STATE OF ILLINOIS   )
)'
COUNTY OF ST. CLAIR   )

I, _____, a Notary Public in and for said County in the State aforesaid, do hereby certify that _____personally known to me to be the same person whose name is subscribed to the within instrument of writing, appeared before me this day in person and acknowledged that she signed the same as her free and voluntary act, for the uses and purposes therein set forth.

Given under my hand and notarial seal this _____ day of _____, 201____.

_____

Notary Public

See Appendix A for a sample Marital Settlement Agreement.

Line-by-Line Analysis:
Joint Parenting Agreement

JOINT PARENTING AGREEMENT

The following is submitted to the court by agreement of the Plaintiff, Rose Smith hereafter referred to as "Mother" and Defendant, Richard Smith, hereafter referred to as "Father", as a proposed plan for the sharing of custodial and child care responsibilities pursuant to, and in compliance with the purposes of the Illinois Marriage and Dissolution of Marriage Act as set forth in Section 102 thereof and in accordance with the procedures set forth in Section 602 of that Act. The parties agree to the following terms of this plan, which is to be incorporated in a subsequent Judgment for Dissolution of Marriage, the terms are as follows:

Identification of Parties

Like the marital settlement agreement (MSA), the joint parenting agreement (JPA) begins by identifying the parties. In the example herein, the parties remain the fictitious, but infamous, Rose and Richard Smith. Rose remains the plaintiff. The parties have two children, John and Susan Smith, in this example.

Both the plaintiff and the defendant are identified initially by name and thereafter by either "mother" or "father." Again, such monikers do not sound as artfully pled as "plaintiff" and "defendant," but such designations lend to the readability of the document for the litigants during negotiations, as well as for later reference months and years after the entry of these agreements.

Additionally, in a JPA, both parents technically have "custody," but no "visitation." Anytime a parent is in possession of the child(ren), he or she is exercising custodial periods. However, the terms custody and visitation are relatively universally understood, while "custodial periods" can cause a layperson some consternation. Thus, once joint parenting is established, the terms custody, custodial periods, and visitation are used somewhat interchangeably. This is not to confuse, but rather to help both parties and any other layperson comprehend the various nuances of each role.

> **1. JOINT CUSTODY. It is acknowledged that both parties are fit and proper persons to have the joint legal care, custody, control, and education of the minor children of the parties, namely:**

Children's Names	Ages	Date of Birth
John Smith	**8**	**10/22/2002**
Susan Smith	**5**	**12/13/2004**

> **The parties further agree that they shall have the joint legal custody of the children but that the permanent physical care, custody, control, and place of principal residence for the children shall be with the Mother.**

In a JPA, both parties are recognized as fit and proper to have custody. Rarely, however, is it advisable to have no designation for a primary residential custodian. So the acknowledgment is made as to joint parenting for the children in question followed by, in this case, the mother as primary parent. As primary parent, or custodial parent, the mother will be responsible for taking the lead in the day-to-day decision-making for the children. However, the primary parent must still comply with the terms of this agreement for extraordinary decisions, as is later set forth in this agreement.

Additionally, her residence is then generally accepted as the permanent residence of the children. This is particularly important in selection of school district. Often a school district will require a copy of this document to verify residency requirements when enrolling the children. This issue was touched on in the MSA section of this book as one of the reasons to separate the marital settlement agreement from the parenting agreement.

We further agree that joint parenting is best facilitated by close proximity of both parents to the children so as to maximize the children's time with both parents. Therefore, we agree that Rose Smith shall not change the primary and legal residence from the _____ school district unless the parties agree in writing. Any request for change shall be decided in accordance with the following provisions relating to dispute resolutions set forth below.

Rarely does a parent, particularly the non-custodial parent, wish to see a great physical distance between himself or herself and the children. So if the parties can agree to a geographical limitation on relocation, the above language can be used to ensure both close proximity and continuity for the children as to attendance in a particular school district.

Parties should be advised that this paragraph is not an absolute bar to moving, but can be used as an additional safeguard for the non-custodial parent if the issue of either a school district change or relocation becomes an issue to be "jointly parented" pursuant to the later sections of the agreement.

2. **ACCESS TO MEDICAL RECORDS AND SCHOOL INFORMATION.** Both parties shall participate actively in raising and guiding the children. To that end, the parties shall share all information in connection with medical, dental, and psychological needs as well as the children's education and progress in school. Both parties shall sign the necessary forms for Medical and School records for the children and such records shall be made available to both parents. Each parent shall be notified of consultations and invited to confer with teachers, counselors, or medical professionals concerning education and health care.

Shared Information

Divorcing parties rarely get along well; if they did, they would probably not be divorcing. Thus, it is advisable to memorialize those areas in which they will continue to communicate. Further, many states have specific statutory rights that continue for both parents, whether custodial or non-custodial. By setting forth in this signed documentation confirmation of access to information, neither party need carry around a copy of the statutes granting them access to the child's medical and school records. Further, the institutions involved with the children, medical or educational, also need not be overly concerned with privacy issues.

> **3. EMERGENCIES AND MEDICATIONS. In case of emergency, where time does not allow consultation with the other parent, the parent with the physical custody (possession) of the children shall take whatever emergency action is necessary to meet the health care or other need. As soon as possible thereafter, the parent making such an emergency decision will advise the other parent of the same. We agree to inform each other of any medical or health problems which may have arisen while either has had custody of the children. We shall provide each other with any medications which the children is taking at the time of transfer of custody and with sufficient information to allow the parent assuming physical custody to obtain refills of that medication.**
>
> **ADDITIONALLY, IF A CHILD IS ON MEDICATIONS, TEMPORARILY – AS IN ANTIBIOTICS, OR PERMANENT – SUCH AS INSULIN, THE PARENTS MUST PROVIDE EACH OTHER WITH SAID MEDICINE OR THE PRESCRIPTION TO REFILL SUCH MEDICINE AT ANY TRANSFER OF CUSTODY.**

A common concern, although not typically realistic, is that if the parents must jointly make major decisions, the child may be at risk in an emergency.

This contingency is therefore expressly covered to allow either parent, regardless of custodial designation, the right to take all necessary emergency action. Immediately thereafter, however, the parent taking such action needs to inform the other of the action taken. Any action of major consequence after the emergency is abated would then be subject to the constraints of the joint parenting rules.

A typical example is as follows: The child, while riding his bicycle, falls and breaks his leg. A trip to the emergency room is warranted, and the parent in possession of the child should obviously take all necessary action to stabilize the condition. If a simple cast is all that is required, and the crisis is over, notification is all that is required to the other party. However, if after the hospital has examined and stabilized the leg, it is determined additional action is necessary, such as extensive reconstruction or amputation, the parties *must* make such a decision jointly.

> **4. JOINT DECISIONS. Both parents acknowledge that in matters of major concern, including but not limited to education, religious training, extraordinary medical care, and extracurricular activities, the parties will consult with each other and make every effort to reach vital decisions jointly. As the physical custodian, the Mother shall apprize the Father of the necessity of making such a vital decision, and the Father shall do likewise when the need for a decision arises while the children are in his physical possession. In the event the parties do not agree as to a decision regarding areas of major concern, the parties shall submit their dispute to mediation as set forth in paragraph 13 below.**

Joint Custody

So many battles are fought, so many feelings are hurt, and so many large attorney fees are incurred over the designation between sole and joint custody. While there are valid reasons for the fight over a designation of joint custody versus sole custody, this is not the venue for a comprehensive discourse of such issues.

Instead, parties entering into a joint parenting agreement have arguably had the benefit of counsel and understand the differences. Suffice it to say joint custody is about decision-making in areas of major concern. Parties should be cautioned that it is not a negotiation regarding all decisions. The crux of the JPA is found in Paragraph 4 above. The parties must consult with each other regarding areas of major concern, including but not limited to education, religious training, extraordinary medical care, and extracurricular activity.

To avoid later contest, it is prudent to advise each party that education in a JPA does not mean whether homework should be done before or after supper, but rather substantive issues, such as the school district of attendance, whether the child should be held back a year, or whether a tutor be hired. Medical issues are typically not whether a cold should be treated with antibiotics, but the substantial issues, such as whether the tonsils should be removed, whether the child should be on ADHD medication, and so on. Religious issues usually do not warrant mediation of attendance at one church or another, but whether the child is raised in mutually exclusive religions or none at all. Finally, extracurricular activities will likely be dictated by the child's interest, unless there is a significant imposition on one or both of the parties' custodial periods. The extreme example, however, is that of an inherently dangerous activity, such as hang gliding.

Finally, the primary custodian is usually—but not necessarily—the party to take the lead in the day-to-day decisions and is therefore most likely to bring to the attention of the other party a need to make a vital or major decision. As long as the parties discuss the issue and agree, the joint parenting provision is satisfied. However, if an agreement cannot be reached, no decision is to be made until mediation is attempted. If mediation fails, the court may need to make the decision for the parties. Additional provisions for the mediation process are contained in Section 13.

> **5. REMOVAL OF CHILDREN FROM THE STATE OF ILLINOIS. The parties agree that neither parent will permanently remove the residence of the children from the State of Illinois without the written agreement of the other parent or permission of the court based on the best interest and welfare of the children.**

Removal

Most states have adopted the Uniform Child Custody Jurisdiction and Enforcement Act (UCCJEA), so the issue of competent jurisdiction for current and future enforcement is only a statute book away. Additionally, many states have laws inclusive of, or in addition to, the UCCJEA that limit the removal of the child. Unfortunately, the typical client is not well versed in these statutory requirements.

Section 5, above, restates in plain language the Illinois statute prohibiting permanent removal of the minor children from the state of Illinois without written agreement of the other parent or approval of court.

However, if the parties have otherwise agreed to removal, the specifics should be included so that the statutory prohibition against removal without court approval is not invoked later by the non-custodial parent.

ALTERNATIVE PROVISION

5. REMOVAL OF CHILDREN FROM THE STATE OF ILLINOIS. The parties agree that the Mother may remove the child from the State of Illinois to the State of California without further written consent or permission of the court. The parties further agree that this joint parenting agreement and subsequent order shall be enrolled in the State of California for all future enforcement issues.

6. VISITATION. The Father shall have visitation rights with the child as the parties agree but, at a minimum, shall include the following:

Visitation

Since this is a *joint parenting* agreement, the parties each have rights to custodial periods. However, for convenience and understanding, it is titled "visitation." This section sets forth the custodial/visitation periods for the non-primary parent, Richard Smith. It should be understood that all periods not specifically set forth for the father in this section are the custodial periods for the mother (unless otherwise further set forth).

This schedule is one that should be used as the underlying timetable, subject to any deviation agreed to by the parties. The parties need to understand that, if made by agreement, any deviation is acceptable, but not necessarily enforceable. When the parties cannot agree, this schedule is the ultimate arbiter. Additionally, the parties do need to have a schedule they can rely on for making vacation plans or other plans wherein they can be assured of time with the children.

The example below sets forth a standard visitation schedule typical in the state of Illinois. Although this schedule is in no way codified, many state courts have a similar schedule available in a fill-in-the-blank format. Other schedules can be as complex as alternating two-day periods (on a seven-day per week schedule) or as simple as alternating weeks with the exchange of custody every Sunday evening with no holidays accounted for.

As with any enforceable order, it is advisable to make the schedule as specific as possible. A comprehensive example is below for parties who remain in relatively close geographical proximity. A schedule for parties residing a substantial distance apart is provided in Appendix C.

> **A. WEEKLY AND WEEKEND VISITATION: The Father shall have visitation every Wednesday from 5:00 p.m. until 9:00 a.m. (or at the beginning of school) on Thursday and on alternate weekends from 5:00 p.m. on Friday until 5:00 p.m. Sunday beginning the 1st weekend after the entry of the Dissolution of Marriage.**

A visitation schedule that alternates periods, such as weekends, should have an identifiable start date, such as the first weekend after the entry of dissolution of marriage. Thus, if enforcement becomes an issue, one only need look to a calendar and count weekends.

B. LEGAL OR SCHOOL HOLIDAYS:

The Parties will also receive the following visitation on legal or school holidays where the children attend or reside beginning at 9:00 a.m. and ending at 6:00 p.m. (or unless otherwise specified). In the event that a party is exercising weekend visitation and a holiday as set forth below is on a Friday or Monday immediately before or after said weekend, the parent exercising custody/visitation shall be entitled to keep the children overnight between the holiday and weekend period.

The Father shall have the following schedule:

Even Numbered Years	Odd Numbered Years
New Year's Day	Martin Luther King's Birthday
Good Friday	President's Day
Memorial Day	Independence Day- 9am to 9am on July 5th
Labor Day	Columbus Day
Veterans' Day	Thanksgiving Day
Christmas Day	Halloween - 9am to 9pm

The Mother shall have the following schedule:

Odd Numbered Years		Even Numbered Years
New Year's Day		Martin Luther King's Birthday
Good Friday		President's Day
Memorial Day		Independence Day- 9am to 9am on July 5th
Labor Day		Columbus Day
Veterans' Day		Thanksgiving Day
Christmas Day		Halloween 9am to 9pm

The holiday schedule is important for a number of reasons. First, the children are likely out of school on all federal holidays, and the parents can have additional visitation with the children (everybody loves a three-day weekend). Second, depending on religious affiliation, the holidays may play an important role in the rearing of the child. Finally, by setting forth an alternating schedule, both parents are guaranteed involvement throughout the children's lives.

C. VACATIONS: The parties will also receive the following visitation during summer vacation, winter vacation (or Christmas break), spring break (or Easter break) as herein specified:

There is some overlap in Section C with that of Section B, above. When drafting any negotiated changes into the schedule, care needs to be given that you do not create an internal conflict. Obviously, if the father has Independence Day as his holiday, as set forth above, nothing should prevent him from including that day along with the summer visit. Alternatively, if it is not his Independence Day, he cannot "trump" the mother's holiday during her selected weeks.

In the example above, the general term of "vacations" is used to signal not necessarily actual vacations, but the children's vacations from school. The vacation periods should thus be defined by the children's school schedule. Additionally, the language used states *where the child resides or attends* to allow the parents to utilize a definitive schedule if the child is not yet of school age or is home schooled.

1. Summer Vacation:

The Father will receive two (2) consecutive weeks of vacation during the summer as celebrated in the schools in the community where the child resides or attends not to interfere with any holidays set forth in Paragraph B above. Visitation shall begin at 6:00 p.m. on the selected Friday and ending on the second succeeding Friday at 6:00 p.m. The Father shall provide no less than thirty (30) days advance notice of his selected weeks.

The Mother will receive two (2) consecutive weeks each summer vacation as celebrated in the schools in the community where the child resides or attends not to interfere with any holidays set forth in Paragraph B above. Visitation shall begin at 6:00 p.m. on the selected Friday and ending on the second succeeding Friday at 6:00 p.m. The Mother shall provide no less than thirty (30) days advance notice of her selected weeks.

> The Mother's selected weeks shall have precedence in Odd numbered years and the Father's selected weeks shall have precedence in Even numbered years. Each parent shall begin his or her summer vacation periods on his/her regularly scheduled weekend as set forth in "A" above.

Summer vacation is likely the only time either parent can have extended uninterrupted time with the children. It is also the time of family vacations. Anywhere from one week to one-half of the summer is a typical visitation schedule for parents. Sufficient notice provisions should be included to allow parents to make plans, schedule trips, and obtain time off work. However, it should be noted, there is no requirement that a parent actually take the children on a vacation or even take off work to be entitled to exercise his or her summer visitation periods.

The paragraph above regarding thirty-day notice can also be changed to date-specific notification times, such as April 1 and April 15 respectively, to allow the parents more time to select dates or to forestall expected enforcement issues.

(2) Winter or Christmas Vacation:

> The Father shall have visitation Even-numbered years beginning 8:00 a.m. on the first scheduled day of vacation as celebrated in the schools in the community where the child resides or attends and ending December 26 at 7:00 p.m. On odd-numbered years, beginning at 7:00 p.m. December 26 and ending at 8:00 p.m. on the following New Year's Day.

> The Mother shall have visitation Odd-numbered years beginning 8:00 a.m. on

> the first scheduled day of vacation as celebrated in the schools in the community where the child resides or attends and ending December 26 at 7:00 p.m. On Even-numbered years, beginning at 7:00 p.m. December 26 and ending at 8:00 p.m. on the following New Year's Day.

In this example JPA, and specifically in the holiday Section B above, Christmas Eve is not included. It can be, along with any other agreed holiday. However, it is often advisable to alternate not only a given day, but also a child's vacation surrounding such holiday. By including the entire Christmas/holiday break, as set forth above, each parent can have perhaps a more meaningful period with the children for travel, visits with extended family, or other reason.

> **(3) Spring or Easter Vacation:**
>
> **The Father shall have visitation on Even-numbered years beginning at 8:00 a.m. of the first full day of said vacation as celebrated in the schools in the community where the children reside or attends and ending at 9:00 p.m. on the evening before said vacation ends.**
>
> **The Mother shall have visitation on Odd-numbered years beginning at 8:00 a.m. of the first full day of said vacation as celebrated in the schools in the community where the children reside or attends and ending at 9:00 p.m. on the evening before said vacation ends.**

The final vacation period addressed in this section (immediately above) is that of spring break. Some schools combine spring break with Easter, while others have independent breaks. The example, for expedience, combines the two.

D. MISCELLANEOUS: The Father will also be entitled to the following miscellaneous visitation periods:

(1) Father's Day of every year from 8:00 a.m. to 9:00 p.m.;
(2) Father's birthday every year from 8:00 a.m. to 9:00 p.m.;
(3) Child's birthday during even-numbered years from 8:00 a.m. to 9:00 p.m., but only during such hours of that child's birthday that such child is not otherwise attending school or some function thereof.

The Mother will be entitled to retain physical custody of the minor children, irrespective of any provision to the contrary herein, during the following periods:

(1) Mother's Day of every year from 8:00 a.m. to 9:00 p.m.;
(2) Mother's birthday every year from 8:00 a.m. to 9:00 p.m.;
(3) Child's birthday during odd-numbered years from 8:00 a.m. to 9:00 p.m.

Any other important dates, either requested by the parties or not otherwise listed above, should be set forth with specifically, as well. It is important to verify that events such as birthdays do not fall on otherwise designated holidays. For example, the mother's birthday may be July 4, or the child's birthday may occasionally fall on Easter. If such incidents arise, additional provisions should ensure both parents have the opportunity to celebrate such days with the children.

If any of the specific days set forth in B, C, and D of this paragraph conflict with the visitation set forth in A of this paragraph, then the specific provisions set forth in B, C, and D shall be controlling. Additionally,

in the event a visitation period is made unavailable by virtue of serious illness or injury of the children, the parties shall cooperate to implement a reasonable substitute visitation period, bearing in mind the best interest of the children.

In finalizing any visitation schedule, there must be a hierarchy as to the controlling schedule. The paragraph above simply makes the routine visitation subject to any special days or vacations. Assuming all other potentially conflicting dates have been accounted for, no more specifics may be necessary.

Finally, if the visitations are missed due to issues regarding the children, the parties should cooperate to substitute visitation periods, bearing in mind the best interests of the children and the overall schedule above.

7.   MODIFICATION   OF   VISITATION   BY AGREEMENT. The parties, by written agreement, shall have the right to alter, modify, and otherwise arrange for specific visitation periods other than those shown above and on such terms and conditions as are conducive to the best interests and welfare of the children.

Modification by Agreement

The parenting agreement need not be a static document. If the parties can agree to minor deviations orally, and assuming both parties live up to the deviations, no further action usually needs to be taken. If a party does not live up to the agreement, the parties need only return to the specifics of this agreement/order. However, if a permanent or major deviation is sought, additional language is set forth in the paragraph above as to how the parties may accomplish a permanent deviation. The parties should be admonished that if the change is significant enough, a new amended agreement should be completed and registered with the court.

8. TRANSPORTATION.

The Father shall pick up the children at the beginning time for all his physical custody (visitation).

The Mother shall pick up the children at the beginning time for all her physical custody (visitation).

Transportation

Transportation for visitation periods is a vital section for any parenting agreement. By defining the responsibility of each party, much confrontation can be avoided. In the example above, the parties share equally the transportation duties. However, transportation duties may be divided as the parties agree, but any transportation schedule should always be clearly defined in writing.

In the example, the father, if he wants to exercise his custodial periods, must pick up the children. The mother, if she wants to exercise her custodial periods, must pick up the children. By defining transportation in this manner, a party need not be concerned he or she is missing visitation because one of the parties is late. If you are late, it is your loss.

When the distances are greater, the parties may continue to share transportation and meet at a mutually agreed-on location approximately equidistant between households. This is where issues of timeliness for the exchange become more problematic.

Finally, if the parties are so far away that alternative modes of transportation are necessary, additional language regarding costs should be addressed.

9. PARENTAL NOTICE. Each parent agrees to keep the other informed as to the exact place where each of them resides, the phone numbers of their homes and places of employment, and if either parent travels out-of-town for any period of more than (3) days then

such person shall notify the other of his or her destination and shall maintain a cell phone number where he or she can be reached.

Parental Notice

For a parenting agreement to work, a certain level of communication needs to be maintained for both parties' benefit, as well as the children's. The paragraph above is essentially a boilerplate statement regarding notice.

10. CHILD ENDANGERMENT PROHIBITION. Both parents agree that at all times when the children are under their physical care, each shall refrain from placing the children in an environment or exposing the children to activities that may endanger the children's physical, mental, emotional or moral well-being. Both parents agree to avoid controlled substances or excessive use of alcoholic beverages or excessive/inappropriate use of prescription medication when the minor children are in their physical custody.

Endangerment

If the parties are both proper and fit as custodians of the minor children, this paragraph may seem redundant. However, as people change after a divorce, or if there is a pre-existing condition to be taken into consideration, the language above can be a reminder of what behavior is acceptable around the children. Additional language may also be added to account for specific concerns of one or both parents.

11. ADDITIONAL PROVISIONS. The parties shall adhere to the following rules with respect to the custody of and visitation with the minor children;

a) Each parent shall refrain from discussing the conduct of the other parent in the presence of the children except in a laudatory or complimentary way;

b) Under no circumstances shall the question of child support, either as to amount, manner or transmission of payment, be raised in the presence of the children;

c) Visitation with the minor children shall not be withheld because of the non-payment of child support. The payment of child support shall not be withheld because of the refusal of the Principal Residential Custodian to grant visitation to the Non-Principal Residential Custodian;

d) The Principal Residential Custodian shall not threaten to withhold visitation from the Non-Principal Residential Custodian. The Non-Principal Residential Custodian shall not threaten to prevent or delay the return of the children to the Principal Residential Custodian after a period of visitation;

e) The Principal Residential Custodian shall prepare the children both physically and mentally for visitation with the Non-Principal Residential Custodian. The children shall be available at the time mutually agreed upon between the parties for the beginning of visitation;

f) The Non-Principal Residential Custodian shall advise the Principal Residential Custodian as soon as possible if the Non-Principal Residential Custodian is unable to keep a planned visitation with the children;

g) Neither parent shall unreasonably question the children regarding the activities of the other parent;

h) The Non-Principal Residential Custodian shall not visit the children at unreasonable hours;

i) The Non-Principal Residential Custodian shall work with the Principal Residential Custodian to arrange visitation schedules which shall take into account the children's education, athletic and social activities. The Non-Principal Residential Custodian may take the children to appropriately planned activities;

Additional Provisions

The additional provisions section set forth above is often referred to as the "rules." These rules are substantially self-explanatory and routinely boilerplate in nature. However, these rules should be reviewed thoroughly by each party and modified as necessary to accommodate any particular concerns of the parties.

12. SCHOOL INFORMATION AND ACTIVITIES. The parties shall jointly determine where the children shall be enrolled in school and take the necessary action with the school authorities of the schools in which the children are to be enrolled to:

a) List the Non-Principal Residential Custodian as a parent of the children;

b) Authorize the school to release to the Non-Principal Residential Custodian any and all information concerning the children;

c) Insure that the Non-Principal Residential Custodian receives copies of any notices regarding the children.

d) The Principal Residential Custodian shall promptly transmit to the Non-Principal Residential Custodian any information received concerning parent-teacher meetings, school club meetings, school programs, athletic schedules and any other school activities in which the children may be engaged or interested within 14 days of receipt.

e) The Principal Residential Custodian shall promptly, after receipt of same, furnish to the Non-Principal Residential Custodian a photocopy of the children's grade or report card and copies of any other reports concerning the children's status or progress.

f) The Principal Residential Custodian shall, when possible, arrange appointments for parent-teacher conferences at a time when the Non-Principal Residential Custodian can be present and whenever possible they shall be attended by both parents.

School Information and Activities

The rules set forth in Section 11 relate to the parties' interaction. In Section 12, above, rules for the joint parenting of the child's education are set forth. In the spirit of a JPA, both parties must be informed and kept updated to make critical joint decisions regarding education. The terms set forth in Section 12 are primarily the duties of the custodial parent with regard to the non-custodial parent to ensure the non-custodial parent's interaction.

Mandatory Mediation and Review

Section 4, previously discussed, defined the scope of the JPA. Section 13 is the owner's manual. The specifics set forth above obligate the parties to a yearly review and set forth the actions to be taken if a dispute arises under this agreement that the parties cannot resolve between themselves.

The parties should be advised that specific action must be taken before a return to court is warranted. Once a particular issue has become unsolvable between the parties, or a particular issue is anticipated to be of significant import, the party requesting resolution must apprise the other of the issue in writing, including suggested remedies. If the issue is not thus resolved, the parties are to submit the issue to a mediator. Typically, the parties split the cost of the mediator, as this serves as a deterrent to a continuous string of mediated problems, real or anticipated.

Finally, the court, having continuing jurisdiction, may then be petitioned for resolution.

13. DISPUTE RESOLUTION, CHANGE OF CIRCUMSTANCE, AND PERIODIC REVIEW. The parents acknowledge that they are attempting to resolve their differences through-the use of this joint parenting agreement and they recognize that the details herein may require future adjustments and changes to reflect the children's best interest.

The parents also recognize that this joint parenting agreement is a dynamic concept subject to re-evaluation and change based upon a substantial change in circumstances of a parent or child. To determine whether different arrangements might better suit future circumstances, the parents hereby agree and stipulate:

a) This agreement shall be reviewed jointly by us at least on an annual basis;

b) That in the event the parents cannot agree as to a vital non-emergency decision affecting the welfare of the children the Circuit Court of _____ County shall retain continuing jurisdiction to adjudicate any disputed issue. The parties agree, however, that if any conflicts arise between the parents as to any of the provisions of this Joint Parenting Agreement or the implementation thereof, that the complaining parent shall first notify the other parent of the nature of the complaint and both parents shall make reasonable attempts to negotiate a settlement of the conflict.

c) Until the conflict is resolved (either by agreement or judicial ruling) the parent exercising physical custody shall continue to make such day-to-day decisions as may be necessary to protect the best interests of the children, but shall take no action with reference to the area in dispute which would prejudice or take unfair advantage of the other party.

d) Wherever practicable under the circumstances, complaints shall be made in writing and given to or mailed to the other parent. Complaints shall include suggestions for resolutions to the issues raised. The parent receiving the complaint shall respond in writing. The response shall indicate what issues are agreed to and make suggestions for resolution of the remaining issues.

e) If the parties are unable to resolve their conflict within a reasonable period, the parties must submit any such disputed issue or conflict for resolution to an impartial mediator, mutually agreed upon, before applying to the court for relief as to all matters that do not involve serious endangerment of the children's physical, mental, moral, or emotional health. In the event the parties cannot agree as to the mediator, or if the mediation is unsuccessful, or if an immediate and serious endangerment is alleged, a court proceeding may be filed by either party.

f) If the parties choose an impartial mediator they shall attempt to agree to the proportions each shall pay for the mediation services. If the mediation is unsuccessful, the cost of the mediator may be included in a petition for fees and costs in connection with the court proceeding.

Request for Entry and Signatures

Finally, the parties must sign and submit the foregoing for entry with the court. As with the marital settlement agreement, it is advisable that the signature lines include notary endorsement.

> **The parties hereto, on behalf of their minor children, respectfully submit the foregoing Joint Parenting Agreement for this Court's approval and incorporation in the Judgment for Dissolution of Marriage to be entered herein.**

———————————————————

Richard Smith

Subscribed and sworn to before me this _____day of _____, 201__.

———————————————————

Notary Public

———————————————————

Rose Smith

Subscribed and sworn to before me this _____day of _____, 201__.

———————————————————

Notary Public

STAN R. WELLER
The Weller Law Firm
120 West Main Street
Suite 212
Belleville, IL 62220
(618)277-3476
(618)277-1500-FAX

See Appendix B for a sample Joint Parenting Agreement.

Appendix A:
Marital Settlement Agreement

IN THE CIRCUIT COURT
FOR THE TWENTIETH JUDICIAL CIRCUIT
ST. CLAIR COUNTY, ILLINOIS

In Re The Marriage Of:	)	
	)	
RICHARD SMITH,	)	
	)	
Plaintiff,	)	
	)	No.: __11_-D-_123_
and	)	
	)	
ROSE SMITH,	)	
	)	
Defendant .	)	

MARITAL SETTLEMENT AGREEMENT

This Agreement is entered into on the date set forth below by and between the Plaintiff, Rose Smith, hereinafter referred to as "Wife", and the Defendant , Richard Smith, hereinafter referred to as "Husband".

<u>WITNESSETH:</u>

WHEREAS:

A. There is a current dissolution of marriage proceeding pending under Case Number _____-D-____, entitled "<u>In re the Marriage of Rose Smith vs. Richard Smith</u>," and no Final Order has yet been entered in that case.

B. Both parties consider it to be in their best interest to settle between themselves all issues that are currently pending in this matter which arise out of the marital relationship or any other relationship between the parties, including all rights of every kind and nature, whether marital or non-marital, real, personal or mixed, which either of them now has or may later claim to have against the other; the right of either party to receive maintenance, and the payment of attorney's fees and costs.

C. This Agreement is made free of collusion and is not made for the purpose of obtaining or stimulating a dissolution of marriage of the parties; however, the parties stipulate and agree that the dissolution of marriage proceedings now pending in the court aforesaid shall proceed and be heard as an uncontested matter as soon as practicable. The Husband hereby enters his appearance in the above-entitled cause as Defendant therein and expressly waives the necessity of process of summons and consents that the same proceedings may be had herein as fully and with the same force and effect as though he had been duly and regularly served with process of summons therein in the State of Illinois at least thirty (30) days prior to any return date designated by Plaintiff herein or as otherwise provided by law.

D. Each party acknowledges and understands that they have the right to conduct discovery, including, but not limited to; conducting depositions, submitting interrogatories, requesting the production of documents, and a mental or physical examination of the opposing party. Both parties have full knowledge and understanding of the finances of this marriage, including property, liabilities and income. Both parties waive their right to conduct formal discovery in an effort to expedite these proceedings and minimize the expenses associated with this case.

E. Each party has had the opportunity to consult with his or her own attorney and each party acknowledges that he or she is not relying upon advice provided by counsel in evaluating the provisions of this Agreement. Each party expressly states that neither have given or received any promises or considerations other than those set forth herein. Both parties expressly state that they have freely and voluntarily entered into this Agreement free of any duress and coercion with full knowledge of each and every provision, and the consequences thereof.

NOW, THEREFORE, in consideration of the mutual and several promises and undertakings contained herein and for other good and valuable consideration, the receipt and sufficiency of which is mutually acknowledged, the parties do hereby agree as follows.

ARTICLE 1
MAINTENANCE

1.1   In consideration of the various promises, agreements and conditions contained in this Agreement, the Wife hereby waives any and all rights she may have to maintenance from the Husband, past, present and future, pursuant to the laws of the State of Illinois or of any other state or country. The Wife acknowledges that this waiver forever bars her from asserting a claim for maintenance against the Husband.

1.2   In consideration of the various promises, agreements and conditions contained in this Agreement, the Husband hereby waives any and all rights he may have to maintenance from the Wife, past, present and future, pursuant to the laws of the State of Illinois or of any other state or country. The Husband acknowledges that this waiver forever bars his from asserting a claim for maintenance against the Wife.

ALTERNATIVE PROVISION

[(TEMPORARY-REHABILITATIVE MAINTENANCE)

1.1 The Wife shall be awarded temporary maintenance in the amount of $800.00 (eight hundred dollars) per month, commencing the first month after the entry of the dissolution of marriage, payable on the 1st of each month thereafter. Payments shall terminate after 48 monthly installment payments of the above referenced amount, or in the event of the Wife's death, remarriage, cohabitation (conjugal) with another person on a regular basis, or upon any other statutorily defined event.

ALTERNATIVELY: Payments shall terminate after 48 monthly installments irregardless of remarriage, cohabitation (conjugal) with another person on a regular basis, or any other statutorily defined event to provide for the financial rehabilitation of the Wife.

1.2   In consideration of the various promises, agreements and conditions contained in this Agreement, the Husband hereby waives any and all rights he may have to maintenance from the Wife, past, present and future, pursuant to the laws of the State of Illinois or of any other state or country. The Husband acknowledges that this waiver forever bars his from asserting a claim for maintenance against the Wife.]

ARTICLE 2
REAL ESTATE

2.1   The Husband shall be awarded, as his sole and exclusive property, the marital home at 1600 Pennsylvania Ave. HomeTown, Illinois and shall assume responsibility for the indebtedness owed thereon and shall hold harmless the Wife on such indebtedness. Further, he shall pay all mortgage payments in a timely manner until refinance. He shall transfer all utilities solely into his name and shall pay same. The Husband shall be responsible for all real estate bills levied against the property, existing or as to be billed in the future.

2.2   The Husband shall refinance or assume the mortgage on such that the Wife is no longer on any mortgage or indebtedness on said property within one year of the entry of dissolution of marriage. The Wife shall execute a quit claim deed conveying her interest to the Husband to remove her name from said property concurrent with any sale, refinance or assumption of the mortgage.

2.3   In the event Husband fails to refinance the indebtedness so as to remove Wife's name from the indebtedness thereon within one year, or in the event Husband fails to timely pay the mortgage payments, the marital home shall be immediately listed for sale and sold as soon as possible. Upon sale of the marital home the parties shall equally divide the proceeds (or divide equally any deficiency/loss) of the sale after any reasonable and customary closing costs, realtor fees and outstanding mortgages have been paid.

2.4   Unless the parties agree or a court orders otherwise, the property shall not be sold for less than a sum sufficient to cover all mortgages and costs of the sale. The parties shall agree on a real estate agent to list the property. In the event the parties cannot agree on a real estate agent, then they shall each select one real estate agent and those two agents shall confer and select a third real estate agent who will list the property for sale. The parties shall agree on the initial listing price and any reductions in the listing price. However, if the parties cannot agree, the listing agent shall make the decision as to any reductions in the listing price. If an offer to buy is made and the parties cannot agree on whether to accept the offer, they may petition the court for resolution of the issue. The parties shall cooperate to execute any documents necessary to effectuate any of the provisions of this section regarding the marital home.

ALTERNATIVE PROVISION 1

[2.2   The Husband shall refinance or assume the mortgage on such that the Wife is no longer on any mortgage or indebtedness on said property within one year of the entry of dissolution of marriage. Said refinance shall be in an amount sufficient to pay off all existing mortgages and to include funds sufficient to pay to the Wife the sum of thirty-five thousand dollars ($35,000.00) as and for her portion of the marital equity in the property. The Wife shall execute a quit claim deed conveying her interest to the Husband to remove her name from said property concurrent with any sale, refinance or assumption of the mortgage.]

ALTERNATIVE PROVISION 2

[2.1   The marital home located at 1600 Pennsylvania Ave. HomeTown, Illinois shall be immediately listed for sale and sold as soon as possible. Upon sale of the marital home the parties shall equally divide the proceeds (or divide equally any deficiency/loss) of the sale after any reasonable and customary closing costs, realtor fees and outstanding mortgages have been paid.

2.2   Unless the parties agree or a court orders otherwise, the property shall not be sold for less than a sum sufficient to cover all mortgages and costs of the sale. The parties shall agree on a real estate agent to list the property. In the event the parties cannot agree on a real estate agent, then they shall each select one real estate agent and those two agents shall confer and select a third real estate agent who will list the property for sale. The parties shall agree on the initial listing price and any reductions in the listing price. However, if the parties cannot agree, the listing agent shall make the decision as to any reductions in the listing price. If an offer to buy is made and the parties cannot agree on whether to accept the offer, they may petition the court for resolution of the issue. The parties shall cooperate to execute any documents necessary to effectuate any of the provisions of this section regarding the marital home.]

ALTERNATIVE PROVISION 3

[2.1   The parties currently own the marital residence located at 1600 Pennsylvania Ave. HomeTown, Illinois that is to be surrendered in bankruptcy as is anticipated to be filed by both parties. The Husband shall maintain temporary possession of the residence until the property is properly surrendered in bankruptcy. Neither party shall maintain any responsibility for any debt owed thereon nor maintain any ownership interest therein.

2.2   Both parties shall comply with all requirements of the bankruptcy proceedings with regards to the marital home and shall cooperate with any requests of the bankruptcy trustee(s) and mortgage company representatives.]

ARTICLE 3
MARITAL PROPERTY

3.1   The Husband shall be awarded all marital property (not otherwise referenced in this Marital Settlement Agreement) now in his possession as his sole and exclusive property.

3.2   The Wife shall be awarded all marital property (not otherwise referenced in this Marital Settlement Agreement) now in her possession as her sole and exclusive property.

ALTERNATIVE PROVISION – specific items

[3.1   The Husband shall be awarded all marital property (not otherwise referenced in this Marital Settlement Agreement) now in his possession except the items set forth in paragraph 3.2 below.

    3.2   *The Wife shall be awarded the following items currently located in the marital residence:*

    a. King sized bed and mattress and the matching furniture located in the master bedroom.

    b. Formal Dining Room Set (table, 6 chairs, and accessories)

    c. Small brown dresser (located in guest bedroom)

    d. Oak Hutch

    e. Riding lawn mower

    f. The wedding china (floral pattern)

    g. The couch, love seat and end tables from the formal living room

    h. DVD / Surround sound system

    i. The Sony 32 inch flat panel television

    j. The T-Fal cookware set

    k. The washer and dryer

    l. All wall hangings/decorations

    m. A digital copy of all marital/family photos

All items listed above shall be removed from the martial residence within 30 days of the entry of dissolution of marriage. The Husband shall cooperate and assist the Wife in removing said items. Any items not specifically listed above shall remain in the residence and shall be the exclusive property of the Husband. In the event the items listed above have not been removed within the allotted 30 days, said items shall also be deemed to be the sole and exclusive property of the Husband.]

ARTICLE 4
PERSONAL PROPERTY

4.1   The Husband shall be awarded all personal property (not otherwise referenced in this Marital Settlement Agreement) now in his possession as his sole and exclusive property.

4.2   The Wife shall be awarded all personal property (not otherwise referenced in this Marital Settlement Agreement) now in her possession as her sole and exclusive property.

ARTICLE 5
VEHICLES

5.1   The Wife shall be awarded the 2003 Jeep Wrangler and the 2006 Coleman Camper as her sole and exclusive possession and shall assume responsibility for the indebtedness owed thereon and shall hold harmless the Husband on such indebtedness. The Wife shall refinance and re-title said vehicles within six (6) months of the entry of dissolution of marriage removing the Husband from any incidents of ownership thereon.

5.2   The Husband shall be awarded the 2004 Ford F150 and the 2007 Triumph Rocket III as his sole and exclusive possession and shall assume responsibility for the indebtedness owed thereon and shall hold harmless the Husband on such indebtedness. The Husband shall refinance and re-title said vehicles within six (6) months of the entry of dissolution of marriage removing the Wife from any incidents of ownership thereon.

5.3   Each party shall sign all necessary documents, titles or loan documents to effectuate the transfer and refinance of the above referenced vehicles.

ARTICLE 6
MARITAL DEBTS

6.1   The Wife shall assume responsibility for all indebtedness owed in her name and she shall hold harmless the Husband on such indebtedness.

6.2   The Husband shall assume responsibility for all indebtedness owed in his name and he shall hold harmless the Wife on such indebtedness.

6.3   There are no jointly held marital debts.

6.4   Each party shall be solely responsible to pay any and all debts and liabilities which he or she has incurred since the date (insert date) of the parties' separation, any debts secured by any property awarded to that party and all debts in his or her own name, including debts not named herein. Each party shall indemnify and hold the other harmless from or against any liability for those debts, including the payment of the other's attorney's fees and costs associated with the default on any such debt.

ALTERNATIVE PROVISION

[6.1   The Wife shall assume responsibility for all indebtedness owed in her name except the debts set forth in paragraph 6.2 below and she shall hold harmless the Husband on such indebtedness.

6.2   The Husband shall assume responsibility for all indebtedness owed in his name and the jointly held marital debts, namely:

a) The CitiBank Visa account ending 4545
b) The Bank of America MasterCard account ending 7878
c) The Home Depot account ending 1010

The debts set forth in paragraph a) b) and c) above are in lieu of maintenance and shall not be dischargeable in bankruptcy. The Husband shall indemnify and hold harmless the Wife on the indebtedness set forth herein.]

ARTICLE 7
PERSONAL DEBTS

7.1   The Husband shall be responsible for all debts currently in his name, including his student loans, and shall hold harmless the Wife on such indebtedness.

7.2   The Wife shall be responsible for all debts currently in her name and shall hold harmless the Husband on such indebtedness.

ARTICLE 8
BANKRUPTCY

8.1   Both parties agree and understand that either party may file bankruptcy. In the event that either party (or both) file bankruptcy, neither party shall be bound by the terms of indemnification as set forth herein. Both parties agree to cooperate with any bankruptcy court or trustee and each other regarding a bankruptcy filing for either/both parties.

8.2   Both parties agree and understand that all debts and liabilities set forth herein, unless otherwise specifically identified, are not "in the form of" or "in lieu of" maintenance or child support and therefore are specifically acknowledged as being dischargeable in bankruptcy.

ARTICLE 9
FINANCIAL ACCOUNTS

9.1   The Husband shall be awarded as his sole and exclusive property the proceeds of all financial accounts maintained in his name, except as otherwise set forth in this Marital Settlement Agreement.

9.2   The Wife shall be awarded as her sole and exclusive property the proceeds of all financial accounts maintained in her name, except as otherwise set forth in this Marital Settlement Agreement.

9.3   There are no joint accounts.

ARTICLE 10
PENSION AND RETIREMENT PLANS

10.1   The Husband shall be awarded all his pension and retirement benefits, vested and contingent, and all such future retirement accounts free of any claim of the Wife. The Husband waives all rights to Wife's pension and retirement benefits, vested, contingent and future.

10.2   The Wife shall be awarded all her pension and retirement benefits, vested and contingent, and all such future retirement accounts free of any claim of the Husband. The Wife waives all rights to Husband's pension and retirement benefits, vested, contingent and future.

10.3   Both parties shall sign any necessary releases of rights to benefits of said plans upon the entry of the dissolution of marriage.

ALTERNATIVE PROVISIONS 1 – General Marital Division

[10.1 The Husband shall be awarded all his pension and retirement benefits, vested and contingent, and all such future retirement accounts free of any claim of the Wife except to the extent set forth below regarding his A.G. Edwards 401k and his Pipe Fitters Union retirement account. The Husband waives all rights to Wife's pension and retirement benefits, vested, contingent and future.

10.2 The Wife shall be awarded all her pension and retirement benefits, vested and contingent, and all such future retirement accounts free of any claim of the Husband. The Wife waives all rights to Husband's pension and retirement benefits, vested, contingent and future except her marital portion of his A.G. Edwards 401k and his Pipe Fitters Union retirement account set forth in paragraphs 10.3 and 10.4 below.

10.3 The Wife shall be awarded 80% of the Husband's A.G. Edwards 401k account as valued on the date of the dissolution of marriage. Said division is an offset to the Wife's marital equity in the marital home awarded to the husband in Section 2 above. It is mutually understood that there has been no withdrawals or loans on said account as of the date of this instrument by either party. Additionally, neither party shall take any action with regard to the 401k account until the entry of the Dissolution of Marriage. The parties shall cooperate in the transfer of said funds. The Wife shall be responsible for the preparation and entry of any forms, Qualified Domestic Relations Orders or any other documentation necessary for the transfer. The transfer shall be completed within six (6) months of the entry of the Dissolution of Marriage Order. The Wife shall be responsible for any cost associated with the transfer including any tax consequences if the funds are withdrawn and not placed with another qualified tax exempt account.]

ALTERNATIVE PROVISIONS 2 - Military

[10.1 The Husband shall be awarded all his pension and retirement benefits, vested and contingent, and all such future retirement accounts free of any claim of the Wife except to the extent set forth below regarding his Thrift Savings Plan and his Military Retirement. The Husband waives all rights to Wife's pension and retirement benefits, vested, contingent and future.

10.2 The Wife shall be awarded all her pension and retirement benefits, vested and contingent, and all such future retirement accounts free of any claim of the

Husband. The Wife waives all rights to Husband's pension and retirement benefits, vested, contingent and future except her marital portion of his Thrift Savings Plan and his Military Retirement as set forth in the remaining paragraphs of this section.

10.3   The Wife shall be awarded $25,000.00 (twenty five thousand dollars) as her portion of the Husband's Thrift Savings Plan (TSP) account. Additionally, neither party shall take any action with regard to the TSP account until the entry of the Dissolution of Marriage. The parties shall cooperate in the transfer of said funds. The Wife shall be responsible for the preparation and entry of any forms, Qualified Domestic Relations Orders or any other documentation necessary for the transfer. The transfer shall be completed within six (6) months of the entry of the Dissolution of Marriage Order. The Wife shall be responsible for any cost associated with the transfer including any tax consequences if the funds are withdrawn and not placed with another qualified tax exempt account.

10.4   The Wife shall be awarded a monthly percentage share of Husband's United States Air Force retainer/retired pay upon Husband's retirement from the United States Air Force. Said award shall be in accordance with and construed by the Uniformed Services Former Spouses' Protection Act of September 8, 1982 (public law 97-252). Wife's monthly percentage share shall be determined by the following formula:

$$\frac{\text{Number of months married while the husband was in the service while obtaining creditable time}}{\text{Total number of months the Husband is/was in the service obtaining creditable time.}} \quad X \quad \tfrac{1}{2} \quad = \quad \text{Wife's portion of the retirement benefit}$$

Disposable military retired/retainer pay as used herein means Husband's gross military retired/retainer pay less only those amounts properly withheld for Federal, State and local income taxes. The share of the disposable military retired/retainer pay shall commence upon the Husband's receipt of the retired/retainer pay and shall continue until the death of either party. OR The Husband and Wife shall select the Surviving Spouse Benefit Plan (SBP) and the Wife shall be identified as the recipient of the SBP benefit. The cost of the SBP shall be deducted from the Husband's OR Wife's portion of his OR her retirement benefit. The Wife will OR will not be entitled to Cost Of Living Allowances (COLA).

10.5   Under the terms of the Uniformed Services Former Spouses' Protection Act, the United States Air Force as the paying authority is required to directly pay Wife her monthly percentage share of Husband's monthly disposable military retired/retainer pay because of the following: **In the course of the parties' marriage, Husband performed at least ten (10) years of service creditable in determining his eligibility for retired/retainer pay.** *The parties were married on April 1, 1998, and divorced on   (enter date of entry of Dissolution)   , 201___. Husband began service creditable in determining his eligibility for retired/retainer pay with the United States Air Force on   (enter date Husband began creditable service   , has performed continuous creditable service since then and is now on active duty with the United States Air Force. Husband's full name and social security number are: Richard Smith, XXX-XX-1234. Wife's full name and social security number are: Rose Smith, XXX-XX-4321.*

10.6   The court finds that the Husband' military retired/retainer pay is and shall be accruing as a result of his service in the United States Air Force and that the military retired/retainer pay is marital property subject to equitable division by the family court of the Circuit Court of St. Clair County, Illinois, pursuant to Illinois Statutes. The court further finds that it is competent to divide the parties' marital property incident to their divorce pursuant to Illinois law. The court finally finds that it has jurisdiction over the Husband for the purpose of dividing his disposable military retired/retainer pay because the Husband has consented to the court's jurisdiction to divide his disposable military are retired/retainer pay.

10.7   Husband has been afforded his rights under the Soldiers' and Sailors Civil Relief Act of 1940 (50 U.S.C. Appendix 501-591).

10.8   The court shall retain jurisdiction over Husband's military retired/retainer pay for so long as the parties both shall live. The court shall also have the authority to make every just and equitable order not inconsistent with the other provisions herein, and not inconsistent with the Uniformed Services Former Spouses' Protection Act or any other applicable law. The court shall also have specific authority to make any orders it deems just and equitable as a result of the income tax consequences which flow from the division and distribution of the retired/retainer pay.

10.9   The court shall also have continuing jurisdiction to make every order reasonably necessary to implement and accomplish the direct payment to Wife by the United States Air Force of her percentage share of Husband's disposable military retired/retainer pay, including the right to advise the United States Air Force of the precise amount or percentage of Husband's disposable military retired/retainer pay to be payable to Wife.]

ARTICLE 11
PERSONAL INJURY CLAIM / LAWSUITS

11.1   The Husband has a personal injury claim now pending in the State of Illinois against Metro Transit Authority. The settlement or award shall be divided such that the Husband shall be awarded 75% of the proceeds after all outstanding liens, costs, expenses of litigation and attorney fees are assessed. The Wife shall be awarded 25% of any settlement or award after all outstanding liens, costs, expenses of litigation and attorney fees are assessed.

11.2   The Wife has a loss of consortium claim pending as part of the Husband's claim now pending against the Metro Transit Authority. The settlement or award shall be divided such that the Wife shall be awarded 75% of the proceeds after all outstanding liens, costs, expenses of litigation and attorney fees are assessed. The Husband shall be awarded 25% of any settlement or award after all outstanding liens, costs, expenses of litigation and attorney fees are assessed.

ARTICLE 12
BUSINESS INTERESTS

12.1   The Husband shall be awarded all interest and stock in the Corporation known as "Smith Carpentry, Inc." as incorporated in the State of Illinois as his sole and exclusive property. The Husband shall be awarded the Corporation and all its assets and inventory, including but not limited to, a Ford F250 pickup truck, all tools and equipment necessary for the ordinary course of business, and the bank accounts held in the corporation's name at Regions Bank.

12. 2   The Wife shall sign and transfer all stock certificates held by her to the Husband within 30 days of the entry of the Dissolution of Marriage and relinquish her position as Vice President via letter of resignation addressed to all shareholders.

ARTICLE 13
PARENTING AGREEMENT

13.1   The parties have voluntarily entered into a Parenting Agreement regarding the custody and visitation of their child(ren) which is to be made part of this Marital Settlement Agreement and entered as part of the final Dissolution of Marriage Order. The parties each believe said Parenting Agreement is fair, equitable and in the best interest of the minor child(ren).

ARTICLE 14
CHILD SUPPORT

14.1   The Husband agrees that he will pay to the Wife, the sum of $800.00 per month beginning on the first day of _____, 201___ and continuing on or before the first (1ˢᵗ) day of each month thereafter as child support until such time as the children have attained the age of nineteen (19) or graduated from high school, whichever comes first. The parties affirm that said amount is a deviation from the statutory guideline of 32% of the Husband's statutory net income. Said deviation is due to the time each parent will share with the children and the respective incomes of each party. Additionally, the parties acknowledge that child support is always modifiable and may be adjusted upon request of either party. Any modification shall be made by the court taking into account all applicable statutory provisions.

ADDITIONAL PROVISION:

[*Additionally, the husband shall each pay ½ (one-half) of the Private School tuition for the years Kindergarten through 12ᵗʰ grade and ½ (one-half) of the necessary educational expenses incurred by the children until graduation from High School. The Wife will pay the fees initially and submit the receipts to the Husband within 10 days. The Husband will reimburse the Wife within 21 days. The Husband will also pay ½ (one-half) of the children's extra circular fees for each child at the beginning of each season/ activity fee period.*]

14.2   Payments shall be made by Order of Withholding through the State Disbursement Unit. The Wife shall prepare a withholding order and serve same upon the Husband's employer within 7 days of the entry of Dissolution of Marriage. The Husband shall apprize the Wife of any change in employment within 14 days of said change and provide all necessary contact information for his employer.

14.3   Payments of child support shall be made directly to the Wife by the Husband by Check or Money Order. In the event that the Husband obtains alternate employment or otherwise becomes more than thirty (30) days late in his child support obligation, the Wife may immediately serve his employer or the Husband individually a withholding order requiring all future payments be made through the State Disbursement Unit.

14.4   The Wife shall claim the minor child, Gwen Smith, on all subsequent tax filings made to the Federal and State Government until it is no longer economically feasible.

14.5   The Husband shall claim the minor child, George Smith, on all subsequent tax filings made to the Federal and State Government until it is no longer economically feasible.

14.6   The parties shall alternate claiming the minor child, Sidney Smith, on subsequent tax filings made to the Federal and State Government, such that the Wife claims the minor child for even numbered years beginning the tax year 2010 (as to be filed April 15, 2011) and the Husband shall claim the minor child for odd numbered years beginning the tax year 2011 (as to be filed April 15, 2012). The parties shall continue alternating claiming said child until it is no longer economically feasible.

14.7   Both parties shall sign any necessary documents and submit same to the Internal Revenue Service to allow the parties to claim the minor children subject the division set forth above.

ARTICLE 15
HEALTH INSURANCE/MEDICAL BILLS

15.1   The Husband shall maintain health insurance for the benefit of the minor child. He shall furnish the Wife with an insurance card and update her timely of any benefit changes or change in providers.

15.2   The Wife shall pay any uncovered expenses (co-pay expenses) at the time of treatment and shall furnish proof of payment to the Husband within 30 days of such treatment. The Husband shall reimburse the Wife one-half (1/2) of said expense within 14 days.

15.3   Any medical, dental, optical, psychiatric, orthodontic or prescription expenses incurred on behalf of the child not covered by insurance (after all insurance payments have been applied) shall be divided equally by the parties directly to the provider within 30 days unless a payment schedule is arranged through said provider.

15.4   If either party intentionally (excluding emergency treatment) seeks treatment for the children outside the policy providers under the Husband's insurance plan, that party shall be solely responsible for uncovered costs.

ARTICLE 16
COLLEGE EXPENSES

16.   The parties agree that the issues of college expenses for the minor children are hereby reserved.

16.1   The Husband agrees that he will pay 50% of the vocational school, college or university education for the child(ren) of the parties, which obligation is predicated upon the scholastic aptitude of each child.

16.2   The Wife agrees that she will pay 25% for the vocational school, college or university education for the child(ren) of the parties, which obligation is predicated upon the scholastic aptitude of each child.

16.3   The child attending such vocational school, college or university shall be responsible for the remaining 25% of the costs of his or her education.

16.4   Decisions affecting the post secondary education of the children, including the choice of the school to be attended, shall be made jointly by the parties and shall consider the expressed preference of the child. Neither party shall unreasonably withhold his or her consent to the expressed preference of the child. In the event the parties are unable to agree upon the school to be attended or upon any of the foregoing, then a court of competent jurisdiction shall make the determination upon proper notice and petition.

16.5   The parties agree that college expenses shall be defined as all the costs and expenses necessarily incurred while pursuing said education, including but not limited to, college application fees, tuition, room and board, books, laboratory and activity fees, clothing, transportation expenses, student health fees, and any other expense usually or ordinarily incurred in the acquisition of a vocational school, college or university education for a period of up to 5 years of attendance at said school(s).

16.6   The Husband's and Wife's obligation to continue payment except those already incurred as set forth in paragraph 16.6 shall immediately terminate in the event that the child fails to maintain at least a C average (3.0 on a 4.0 scale) for more than two semesters, ceases to matriculate (for any reason) at such a vocational, college or university for more than one semester, or by written agreement of the parties.

16.7   Any expenses in the form of student loans or other deferred payment arrangements shall be maintained and paid in the ratio set forth in paragraphs 16.1, 16.2 and 16.3 above as to the entirety of the costs incurred.

ARTICLE 17
INCOME TAXES

17.1   The Husband, Richard Smith, affirmatively states that he has paid his portion of all income taxes, state and federal, on all returns filed by the parties (jointly or separately) during the course of their marriage. The Husband further acknowledges that if additional liability is assessed as a result of the joint or separate tax returns filed by the parties (or amendments thereto), as filed during the course of the marriage, he shall fully indemnify and hold harmless the Wife for any liability, tax deficiency, penalty or interest, together with any costs expended in the defense of any claimed tax deficiency resulting from the filing of said tax returns, by reason of any information set forth on said return which is attributable to his income or his deductions based on information furnished by him on said returns. In the event additional refunds or stimulus payments are paid or received as a result of any tax returns filed while the parties were married, said funds shall be divided pro-rata based on the respective incomes of the parties at the time the return was processed.

17.2   The Wife, Rose Smith, affirmatively states that she has paid her portion of all income taxes, state and federal, on all returns filed by the parties (jointly or separately) during the course of their marriage. The Wife further acknowledges that if additional liability is assessed as a result of the joint or separate tax returns filed by the parties (or amendments thereto), as filed during the course of the marriage, she shall fully indemnify and hold harmless the Husband for any liability, tax deficiency, penalty or interest, together with any costs expended in the defense of any claimed tax deficiency resulting from the filing of said tax returns, by reason of any information set forth on said return which is attributable to her income or her deductions based on information furnished by her on said returns. In the event additional refunds or stimulus payments are paid or received as a result of any tax returns filed while the parties were married, said funds shall be divided pro-rata based on the respective incomes of the parties at the time the return was processed.

17.3   The parties agree and acknowledge that if additional liability is assessed as a result of the joint or separate tax returns filed by the parties (or amendments thereto), during the course of the marriage, as a result of mutual mistake, the parties shall share said liability (including the costs expended in the defense of any claimed tax deficiency) pro-rata based on the respective incomes of the parties at the time the return was processed.

17.4   The parties agree that if it becomes necessary to file amendments to any returns for the years in which the parties where married, they will fully cooperate with each other and the requesting entity, including providing necessary documentation, and authorizing third parties to represent each of them in connection with preparing amended returns or any related issue to said tax filings. The parties shall provide each other with copies of any amended returns as filed.

17.5   The parties agree that the division and transfers of property made pursuant to this Agreement are incident to the divorce of the parties. No gain or loss (capital or otherwise) shall be claimed in connection with the transfer of property or money provided by this Agreement except as to any taxable transfers from qualified retirement plans. The tax basis attributable to all property affected by this Agreement shall remain the tax basis which the property had prior to the dissolution of marriage. The party receiving any property hereunder shall be responsible for any tax liability associated therewith and shall hold the other party harmless from any and all such tax liability including interest and penalties.

17. 6   The parties understand that each must file a separate individual tax return in the forthcoming tax year and that all claims and deductions shall be made consistent with the terms and conditions set forth above.

ARTICLE 18
ATTORNEY'S FEES

18.1   Each party shall pay all of his or her own attorneys' fees and costs incurred in these proceedings and shall indemnify and hold the other harmless with respect thereto.

ALTERNATIVE PROVISION

[18.1   The Husband shall pay all of his attorney fees and hold harmless the Wife with respect thereto. The Husband shall also reimburse the Wife the sum of $3,000.00 as and for a portion of her attorney fees incurred herein. The Husband shall pay said sum directly to the Wife within 60 (sixty) days of the entry of Dissolution of Marriage.]

18.2   Husband and Wife acknowledge that they are fully advised of their right to a full and complete hearing as to their attorneys' fees and costs under the Illinois Marriage and Dissolution of Marriage Act (750 ILCS 5/508), and the right to request the other party's contribution to her of his or her attorney's fees and costs under said Act (750 ILCS 5/503(j)), and have knowingly and voluntarily waived their right to a contribution hearing.

ARTICLE 19
GENERAL PROVISIONS

19.1   Execution of Documents: Each party shall agree to execute and deliver, concurrently with the execution hereof, all documents or instruments necessary to vest the titles and estates in the respective parties hereto as sole and separate ownership and to otherwise carry out the purposes of this Agreement. If either party shall fail or refuse to execute any such documents, then this Agreement shall constitute a full and present transfer, assignment and conveyance of all rights hereinabove designated to be transferred, assigned and conveyed, and a full, present and effective relinquishment and wavier of all rights hereinabove designated to be relinquished and waived. If either party fails for a period of more than 30 days after the effective date of this agreement to make, execute acknowledge or deliver any necessary documents or instruments which are reasonably required to implement the terms of this agreement, a judicial officer of the Circuit Court for the Twentieth Judicial Circuit, St. Clair County, Illinois is hereby authorized to make, execute acknowledge, and deliver such documents and instruments at the request of either party. This authorization includes, but shall not be limited to, any and all documents and instruments pertaining to the transfer or conveyance of real and personal property and beneficiary interests in land trusts.

19.2   Mutual Releases: To the fullest extent permitted by law, and except as otherwise provided herein, each of the parties does hereby forever release, waive and quitclaim all rights of maintenance, alimony, inheritance, descent and distribution, homestead, dower, community interest and all other interest and estate as husband and wife, widow or widower, including any and all right, title, claim or interest which he or she might have or be entitled to claim in, to or against the property, assets and estate of the other, whether real, personal or marital or non-marital, whether community or separate, whether now owned or hereafter in any manner acquired by the other party, whether in possession or in expectancy and whether vested or contingent.

19.3   Construction of Agreement:

A. The recitals set forth at the commencement of this Agreement are intended to be and are made a part of this Agreement.

B. The captions contained in this Agreement are for convenience only and are not intended to limit or define the scope or effect of any provision of this Agreement.

C. Any word in the text of this Agreement shall be read as singular or as plural and as masculine, feminine or neuter gender as may be appropriate under the circumstances to carry out the parties' intent.

D. The provisions of this Agreement except as specifically set forth herein and as to, custody, support or visitation of the child shall not be subject to subsequent modification by any Court, except by mutual written consent of the parties or; except as otherwise set forth above.

E. The provisions of this Agreement contain the entire understanding of the parties. No representations, warranties, promises, covenants or undertakings other than those expressly set forth herein have been made by either party to the other.

F. This Agreement shall be construed under the general laws of the State of Illinois, irrespective of the later domicile or residence of Husband and Wife.

G. It is expressly understood and agreed between the parties that in the event a court of competent jurisdiction at that time after the entry of a Judgment of Dissolution of Marriage holds that a portion of this Agreement is invalid or unenforceable, the remainder hereof shall not be affected thereby and shall continue in full force and effect.

H. This Agreement shall become effective in the event and upon the date a Judgment of Dissolution of Marriage is entered in this cause.

19.4   Indemnity: The term indemnity or indemnify as used in this Agreement shall mean that the party agreeing to indemnify (the "Indemnitor") agrees to secure and save the other party (the "Indemnitee") from potential or actual loss which includes: any and all of Indemnitee's attorneys' fees or other expenses incurred by the Indemnitee in investigating or defending against any claim or for enforcing the provisions of the indemnity.

19.5 <u>Enforcement</u>: In the event either party requires intervention from the Court for enforcement of any provision herein, as a result of a breach or default by the other party, the breaching/defaulting party shall pay the reasonable attorney's fees and costs incurred by the other in connection with such enforcement action.

19.6 <u>Reservation of Rights</u>: Each party reserves the right to prosecute or defend any action now pending or which may hereafter be brought for relief under the Illinois Marriage and Dissolution of Marriage Act.

ARTICLE 20
CLOSING AND SIGNATURES

20.1 Each party agrees that his or her acceptance of the terms set forth in this Agreement represents a full and final settlement of any claims he or she may have in and to any of the property, either marital or non-marital, now owned or hereinafter acquired by his or her spouse, whether real, personal or inadvertently excluded. The parties agree that the distribution of property outlined in this Article is fair and equitable.

20.2 FURTHER, The parties agree that the terms of this Agreement shall be made the Order of this Court if this Agreement is approved by the Court.

Dated: _____   _____

                                                         Richard Smith

STATE OF ILLINOIS   )
)
COUNTY OF ST. CLAIR   )

I, _____, a Notary Public in and for said County in the State aforesaid, do hereby certify that _____, personally known to me to be the same person whose name is subscribed to the within instrument of writing, appeared before me this day in person and acknowledged that he signed the same as his free and voluntary act, for the uses and purposes therein set forth.

Given under my hand and notarial seal this ____ day of _____, 201__.

_____

Notary Public

Dated: _____   _____

Rose Smith

STATE OF ILLINOIS   )

)'

COUNTY OF ST. CLAIR   )

I, _____, a Notary Public in and for said County in the State aforesaid, do hereby certify that _____personally known to me to be the same person whose name is subscribed to the within instrument of writing, appeared before me this day in person and acknowledged that she signed the same as her free and voluntary act, for the uses and purposes therein set forth.

Given under my hand and notarial seal this ____ day of _____, 201____.

_____

Notary Public

Appendix B:
Joint Parenting Agreement

IN THE CIRCUIT COURT
FOR THE TWENTIETH JUDICIAL CIRCUIT
ST. CLAIR COUNTY, ILLINOIS

ROSE SMITH,	)	
	)	
Petitioner,	)	
	)	No.: _11-D-123_
vs.	)	
	)	
RICHARD,	)	
	)	
Respondent.	)	

JOINT PARENTING AGREEMENT

The following is submitted to the court by agreement of the Plaintiff, Rose Smith hereafter referred to as "Mother" and Defendant, Richard Smith, hereafter referred to as "Father", as a proposed plan for the sharing of custodial and child care responsibilities pursuant to, and in compliance with the purposes of the Illinois Marriage and Dissolution of Marriage Act as set forth in Section 102 thereof and in accordance with the procedures set forth in Section 602 of that Act. The parties agree to the following terms of this plan, which is to be incorporated in a subsequent Judgment for Dissolution of Marriage, the terms are as follows:

1. JOINT CUSTODY. It is acknowledged that both parties are fit and proper persons to have the joint legal care, custody, control, and education of the minor children of the parties, namely:

Children's Names	Ages	Date of Birth
John Smith	8	10/22/2002
Susan Smith	5	12/13/2004

The parties further agree that they shall have the joint legal custody of the children but that the permanent physical care, custody, control, and place of principal residence for the children shall be with the Mother.

We further agree that joint parenting is best facilitated by close proximity of both parents to the children so as to maximize the children's time with both parents. Therefore, we agree that Rose Smith shall not change the primary and legal residence from the _____ school district unless the parties agree in writing. Any request for change shall be decided in accordance with the following provisions relating to dispute resolutions set forth below.

2. ACCESS TO MEDICAL RECORDS AND SCHOOL INFORMATION. Both parties shall participate actively in raising and guiding the children. To that end, the parties shall share all information in connection with medical, dental, and psychological needs as well as the children's education and progress in school. Both parties shall sign the necessary forms for Medical and School records for the children and such records shall be made available to both parents. Each parent shall be notified of consultations and invited to confer with teachers, counselors, or medical professionals concerning education and health care.

3. EMERGENCIES AND MEDICATIONS. In case of emergency, where time does not allow consultation with the other parent, the parent with the physical custody (possession) of the children shall take whatever emergency action is necessary to meet the health care or other need. As soon as possible thereafter, the parent making such an emergency decision will advise the other parent of the same. We agree to inform each other of any medical or health problems which may have arisen while either has had custody of the children. We shall provide each other with any medications which the children is taking at the time of transfer of custody and with sufficient information to allow the parent assuming physical custody to obtain refills of that medication.

4. JOINT DECISIONS. Both parents acknowledge that in matters of major concern, including but not limited to education, religious training, extraordinary medical care, and extracurricular activities, the parties will consult with each other and make every effort to reach vital decisions jointly. As the physical custodian, the Mother shall apprize the Father of the necessity of making such a vital decision, and the Father shall do likewise when the need for a decision arises while the children are in his physical possession. In the event the parties do not agree as to a decision regarding areas of major concern, the parties shall submit their dispute to mediation as set forth in paragraph 13 below.

5. REMOVAL OF CHILDREN FROM THE STATE OF ILLINOIS. The parties agree that neither parent will permanently remove the residence of the children from the State of Illinois without the written agreement of the other parent or permission of the court based on the best interest and welfare of the children.

ALTERNATIVE PROVISION

[5. REMOVAL OF CHILDREN FROM THE STATE OF ILLINOIS. The parties agree that the Mother may remove the child from the State of Illinois to the State of California without further written consent or permission of the court. The parties further agree that this joint parenting agreement and subsequent order shall be enrolled in the State of California for all future enforcement issues.]

6. VISITATION. The Father shall have visitation rights with the child as the parties agree but, at a minimum, shall include the following:

A. WEEKLY AND WEEKEND VISITATION: The Father shall have visitation every Wednesday from 5:00 p.m. until 9:00 a.m. (or at the beginning of school) on Thursday and on alternate weekends from 5:00 p.m. on Friday until 5:00 p.m. Sunday beginning the 1st weekend after the entry of the Dissolution of Marriage.
B. LEGAL OR SCHOOL HOLIDAYS: The Parties will also receive the following visitation on legal or school holidays where

the children attend or reside beginning at 9:00 a.m. and ending at 6:00 p.m.(or unless otherwise specified). In the event that a party is exercising weekend visitation and a holiday as set forth below is on a Friday or Monday immediately before or after said weekend, the parent exercising custody/visitation shall be entitled to keep the children overnight between the holiday and weekend period.

The Father shall have the following schedule:

Even Numbered Years		Odd Numbered Years
New Year's Day		Martin Luther King's Birthday
Good Friday		President's Day
Memorial Day		Independence Day- 9am to 9am on July 5th
Labor Day		Columbus Day
Veterans' Day		Thanksgiving Day
Christmas Day		Halloween - 9am to 9pm

The Mother shall have the following schedule:

Odd Numbered Years		Even Numbered Years
New Year's Day		Martin Luther King's Birthday
Good Friday		President's Day
Memorial Day		Independence Day- 9am to 9am on July 5th

Odd Numbered Years		Even Numbered Years
Labor Day		Columbus Day
Veterans' Day		Thanksgiving Day
Christmas Day		Halloween 9am to 9pm

C. VACATIONS: The parties will also receive the following visitation during summer vacation, winter vacation (or Christmas break), spring break (or Easter break) as herein specified:

1. Summer Vacation:

The Father will receive two (2) consecutive weeks of vacation during the summer as celebrated in the schools in the community where the child resides or attends not to interfere with any holidays set forth in Paragraph B above. Visitation shall begin at 6:00 p.m. on the selected Friday and ending on the second succeeding Friday at 6:00 p.m. The Father shall provide no less than thirty (30) days advance notice of his selected weeks.

The Mother will receive two (2) consecutive weeks each summer vacation as celebrated in the schools in the community where the child resides or attends not to interfere with any holidays set forth in Paragraph B above. Visitation shall begin at 6:00 p.m. on the selected Friday and ending on the second succeeding Friday at 6:00 p.m. The Mother shall provide no less than thirty (30) days advance notice of her selected weeks.

The Mother's selected weeks shall have precedence in Odd numbered years and the Father's selected weeks shall have precedence in Even numbered years. Each parent shall begin his or her summer vacation periods on his/her regularly scheduled weekend as set forth in "A" above.

(2) Winter or Christmas Vacation:

The Father shall have visitation Even-numbered years beginning 8:00 a.m. on the first scheduled day of vacation as celebrated in the schools in the community where the child resides or attends and ending December 26 at 7:00 p.m. On odd-numbered years, beginning at 7:00 p.m. December 26 and ending at 8:00 p.m. on the following New Year's Day.

The Mother shall have visitation Odd-numbered years beginning 8:00 a.m. on the first scheduled day of vacation as celebrated in the schools in the community where the child resides or attends and ending December 26 at 7:00 p.m. On Even-numbered years, beginning at 7:00 p.m. December 26 and ending at 8:00 p.m. on the following New Year's Day.

(3) Spring or Easter Vacation:

The Father shall have visitation on Even-numbered years beginning at 8:00 a.m. of the first full day of said vacation as celebrated in the schools in the community where the children reside or attends and ending at 9:00 p.m. on the evening before said vacation ends.

The Mother shall have visitation on Odd-numbered years beginning at 8:00 a.m. of the first full day of said vacation as celebrated in the schools in the community where the children reside or attends and ending at 9:00 p.m. on the evening before said vacation ends.

D. MISCELLANEOUS: The Father will also be entitled to the following miscellaneous visitation periods:

(1) Father's Day of every year from 8:00 a.m. to 9:00 p.m.;
(2) Father's birthday every year from 8:00 a.m. to 9:00 p.m.;
(3) Child's birthday during even-numbered years from 8:00 a.m. to 9:00 p.m., but only during such hours of that child's birthday that such child is not otherwise attending school or some function thereof.

The Mother will be entitled to retain physical custody of the minor children, irrespective of any provision to the contrary herein, during the following periods:

(1) Mother's Day of every year from 8:00 a.m. to 9:00 p.m.;
(2) Mother's birthday every year from 8:00 a.m. to 9:00 p.m.;
(3) Child's birthday during odd-numbered years from 8:00 a.m. to 9:00 p.m.

If any of the specific days set forth in B, C, and D of this paragraph conflict with the visitation set forth in A of this paragraph, then the specific provisions set forth in B, C, and D shall be controlling. Additionally, in the event a visitation period is made unavailable by virtue of serious illness or injury of the children, the parties shall cooperate to implement a reasonable substitute visitation period, bearing in mind the best interest of the children.

7. MODIFICATION OF VISITATION BY AGREEMENT. The parties, by written agreement, shall have the right to alter, modify, and otherwise arrange for specific visitation periods other than those shown above and on such terms and conditions as are conducive to the best interests and welfare of the children.

8. TRANSPORTATION.

The Father shall pick up the children at the beginning time for all his physical custody (visitation).

The Mother shall pick up the children at the beginning time for all her physical custody (visitation).

9. PARENTAL NOTICE. Each parent agrees to keep the other informed as to the exact place where each of them resides, the phone numbers of their homes and places of employment, and if either parent travels out-of-town for any period of more than (3) days then such person shall notify the other of his or her destination and shall maintain a cell phone number where he or she can be reached.

10. CHILD ENDANGERMENT PROHIBITION. Both parents agree that at all times when the children are under their physical care, each shall refrain from placing the children in an environment or exposing the children to activities that may endanger the children's physical, mental, emotional or moral well-being. Both parents agree to avoid controlled substances or excessive use of alcoholic beverages or prescription medication when the minor children are in their physical custody.

11. ADDITIONAL PROVISIONS. The parties shall adhere to the following rules with respect to the custody of and visitation with the minor children;

a) Each parent shall refrain from discussing the conduct of the other parent in the presence of the children except in a laudatory or complimentary way;

b) Under no circumstances shall the question of child support, either as to amount, manner or transmission of payment, be raised in the presence of the children;

c) Visitation with the minor children shall not be withheld because of the non-payment of child support. The payment of child support shall not be withheld because of the refusal of the Principal Residential Custodian to grant visitation to the Non-Principal Residential Custodian;

d) The Principal Residential Custodian shall not threaten to withhold visitation from the Non-Principal Residential Custodian. The Non-Principal Residential Custodian shall not threaten to prevent or delay the return of the children to the Principal Residential Custodian after a period of visitation;

e) The Principal Residential Custodian shall prepare the children both physically and mentally for visitation with the Non-Principal Residential Custodian. The children shall be available at the time mutually agreed upon between the parties for the beginning of visitation;

f) The Non-Principal Residential Custodian shall advise the Principal Residential Custodian as soon as possible if the Non-Principal Residential Custodian is unable to keep a planned visitation with the children;

g) Neither parent shall unreasonably question the children regarding the activities of the other parent;

h) The Non-Principal Residential Custodian shall not visit the children at unreasonable hours;

i) The Non-Principal Residential Custodian shall work with the Principal Residential Custodian to arrange visitation schedules which shall take into account the children's education, athletic and social activities. The Non-Principal Residential Custodian may take the children to appropriately planned activities;

12. SCHOOL INFORMATION AND ACTIVITIES. The parties shall jointly determine where the children shall be enrolled in school and take the necessary action with the school authorities of the schools in which the children are to be enrolled to:

a) List the Non-Principal Residential Custodian as a parent of the children;

b) Authorize the school to release to the Non-Principal Residential Custodian any and all information concerning the children;

c) Insure that the Non-Principal Residential Custodian receives copies of any notices regarding the children.

d) The Principal Residential Custodian shall promptly transmit to the Non-Principal Residential Custodian any information received concerning parent-teacher meetings, school club meetings, school programs, athletic schedules and any other school activities in which the children may be engaged or interested within 14 days of receipt.

e) The Principal Residential Custodian shall promptly, after receipt of same, furnish to the Non-Principal Residential Custodian a photocopy of the children's grade or report card and copies of any other reports concerning the children's status or progress.

f) The Principal Residential Custodian shall, when possible, arrange appointments for parent-teacher conferences at a time when the Non-Principal Residential Custodian can be present and whenever possible they shall be attended by both parents.

13.   DISPUTE   RESOLUTION,   CHANGE   OF CIRCUMSTANCE, AND PERIODIC REVIEW. The parents acknowledge that they are attempting to resolve their differences through the use of this joint parenting agreement and they recognize that the details herein may require future adjustments and changes to reflect the children's best interest.

The parents also recognize that this joint parenting agreement is a dynamic concept subject to re-evaluation and change based upon a substantial change in circumstances of a parent or child. To determine whether different arrangements might better suit future circumstances, the parents hereby agree and stipulate:

a) This agreement shall be reviewed jointly by us at least on an annual basis;

b) That in the event the parents cannot agree as to a vital non-emergency decision affecting the welfare of the children the Circuit Court of _____ County shall retain continuing jurisdiction to adjudicate any disputed issue. The parties agree, however, that if any conflicts arise between the parents as to any of the provisions of this Joint Parenting Agreement or the implementation thereof, that the complaining parent shall first notify the other parent of the nature of the complaint and both parents shall make reasonable attempts to negotiate a settlement of the conflict.

Wherever practicable under the circumstances complaints shall be made in writing and given to or mailed to the other parent. Complaints shall include suggestions for resolutions to the issues raised. The parent receiving the complaint shall respond in writing. The response shall indicate what issues are agreed to and make suggestions for resolution of the remaining issues.

If the parties are unable to resolve their conflict within a reasonable period of time the parties must submit any such disputed issue or conflict for resolution to an impartial mediator, mutually agreed upon, before applying to the Court for relief as to all matters which do not involve serious endangerment of the children's physical, mental, moral or emotional health. In the event the parties cannot agree as to the mediator, or if the mediation is unsuccessful, or if an immediate and serious endangerment is alleged, a court proceeding may be filed by either party.

If the parties choose an impartial mediator they shall attempt to agree to the proportions each shall pay for the mediation services. If the mediation is unsuccessful, the cost of the mediator may be included in a petition for fees and costs in connection with the court proceeding.

c) Until the conflict is resolved (either by agreement or judicial ruling) the parent exercising physical custody shall continue to make such day-to-day decisions as may be necessary to protect the best interests of the children, but shall take no action with reference to the area in dispute which would prejudice or take unfair advantage of the other party.

The parties hereto, on behalf of their minor children, respectfully submit the foregoing Joint Parenting Agreement for this Court's approval and incorporation in the Judgment for Dissolution of Marriage to be entered herein.

Richard Smith

Subscribed and sworn to before me this ___ day of _____, 201__.

_____

Notary Public

_____

Rose Smith

Subscribed and sworn to before me this ___day of _____, 201__.

_____

Notary Public

STAN R. WELLER
The Weller Law Firm
120 West Main Street
Suite 212
Belleville, IL 62220
(618)277-3476
(618)277-1500-FAX

Appendix C:
Local and Long Distance
Visitation Schedule

6. VISITATION. The Father shall have visitation based upon the Mother's location with regards to the minor child as follows:

So long as the Mother and children live within a 100 mile radius of the Father: The Father, shall have visitation rights, as the parties agree, but, at a minimum currently shall include the following:

A. WEEKLY AND WEEKEND VISITATION: The Father shall have visitation every Wednesday from 6:00 p.m. to 8:00 p.m. and alternate weekends from 6:00 p.m. on Friday evening until Sunday evening ending at 6:00 p.m. beginning the 1st weekend after the entry of the Dissolution of Marriage.

B. LEGAL OR SCHOOL HOLIDAYS: The Father will also receive the following visitation on legal or school holidays beginning at 9:00 a.m. and ending at 6:00 p.m. (or unless otherwise specified) of the day specified:

The Father shall have the following schedule:

Even Numbered Years		Odd Numbered Years
New Year's Day		Martin Luther King's Birthday
Washington's Birthday		Lincoln's Birthday
Good Friday		Memorial Day
Labor Day		Independence Day- 9am

Even Numbered Years		Odd Numbered Years
		to 9am on July 5th
Veterans' Day		Columbus Day
Halloween - 9am to 9pm		Thanksgiving Day
Christmas Day		

The Mother shall have the following schedule:

Odd Numbered Years		Even Numbered Years
New Year's Day		Martin Luther King's Birthday
Washington's Birthday		Lincoln's Birthday
Good Friday		Memorial Day
Labor Day		Independence Day- 9am to 9am on July 5th
Veterans' Day		Columbus Day
Halloween 9am to 9pm		Thanksgiving Day
Christmas Day		

C. VACATIONS: The Father will also receive the following visitation during summer vacation, winter vacation (or Christmas break), spring break (or Easter break) as herein specified:

The Father will receive two (2) consecutive weeks of vacation during the summer as celebrated in the schools in the community where the child resides. Visitation shall begin at 6:00 p.m. on the selected Friday and ending on the second succeeding Friday at 6:00 p.m. The Father shall provide no less than thirty (30) days advance notice of his selected weeks.

The Mother will receive two (2) consecutive weeks each summer vacation as celebrated in the schools in the community where the child resides. Visitation shall begin at 6:00 p.m. on the selected Friday and ending on the second succeeding Friday at 6:00 p.m. The Mother shall provide no less than thirty (30) days advance notice of her selected weeks.

The Mother's selected weeks shall have precedence in Even numbered years and the Father's selected weeks shall have precedence in Odd numbered years. Each parent shall begin his or her summer vacation periods on his/her regularly scheduled weekend as set forth in "A" above.

(2) Winter or Christmas Vacation: The Father shall receive visitation for Winter/Christmas vacation on Even-numbered years beginning 8:00 a.m. on the first scheduled day of vacation as celebrated in the schools in the community where the children reside and ending December 26 at 7:00 p.m. On odd-numbered years, beginning at 7:00 p.m. December 26 and ending at 8:00 p.m. on the following New Year's Day. The Mother shall have the alternate schedule.

(3) Spring or Easter Vacation: The Father shall receive visitation for Spring/Easter vacation in Even-numbered years beginning at 8:00 a.m. of the first full day of said vacation as celebrated in the schools in the community where the children reside and ending at 9:00 p.m. on the second evening before said vacation ends. The Mother shall have the alternate schedule.

D. MISCELLANEOUS: The Father will also be entitled to the following miscellaneous visitation periods:

(1) Father's Day of every year from 8:00 a.m. to 9:00 p.m.;

(2) Father's birthday every year from 8:00 a.m. to 9:00 p.m.;

(3) Child's birthday during even-numbered years from 8:00 a.m. to 9:00 p.m., but only during such hours of that child's birthday that such child is not otherwise attending school or some function thereof.

The Mother will be entitled to retain physical custody of the minor children, irrespective of any provision to the contrary herein, during the following periods:

(1) Mother's Day of every year from 8:00 a.m. to 9:00 p.m.;

(2) Mother's birthday every year from 8:00 a.m. to 9:00 p.m.;

(3) Child's birthday during odd-numbered years from 8:00 a.m. to 9:00 p.m.

If any of the specific days set forth in B, C, and D of this paragraph conflict with the visitation set forth in A of this paragraph, then the specific provisions set forth in B, C, and D shall be controlling. Neither party shall have any restriction for travel during any visitation periods.

7. ALTERNATE VISITATION SCHEDULE. If the Mother and children live outside a 100 mile radius of the Father: The Father, shall have visitation rights, as the parties agree, which, at a minimum currently shall include the following:

A. Holiday and Summer visitation:

(1) Summer Vacation: The Father will receive four (4) consecutive weeks of vacation during the summer as celebrated in the schools in the community where the child resides. Visitation shall begin at 6:00 p.m. on the selected Friday and ending on the corresponding Friday (four weeks later) at 6:00 p.m. The Father shall provide no less than thirty (30) days advance notice of his selected weeks.

The Mother will receive four (4) consecutive weeks each summer vacation as celebrated in the schools in the community where the child resides. Visitation shall begin at 6:00 p.m. on the selected Friday and ending on corresponding Friday (four weeks later) at 6:00 p.m. The Mother shall provide no less than thirty (30) days advance notice of her selected weeks.

(2) Winter or Christmas Vacation: Even-numbered years beginning 8:00 a.m. on the first scheduled day of vacation as celebrated in the schools in the community where the child resides and ending December 26 at 7:00 p.m. On odd-numbered years, beginning at 7:00 p.m. December 26 and ending at 8:00 p.m. on the following New Year's Day.

(3) Spring or Easter Vacation: Even-numbered years beginning at 8:00 a.m. of the first full day of said vacation as celebrated in the schools in the community where the child resides and ending at 9:00 p.m. on the evening before said vacation ends.

B. The Father may have additional visitation as the parties agree up to 25 (twenty five) days per calendar year but not to interfere with school attendance, or the holiday and summer schedule as set forth above. The Petitioner's agreement as to the additional visitation shall not be unreasonably withheld. Said days are in addition to the visitation as set forth in 7(1) and 7(2) above and there shall be no other "make up days."

C. LEGAL OR SCHOOL HOLIDAYS: the Father may exercise any visitation as set forth in the schedule contained in paragraph 6(B) above.

D MISCELLANEOUS: The Father will also be entitled to the following miscellaneous visitation periods:

(1) Father's Day of every year from 10:00 a.m. to 7:00 p.m.;
(2) Father's birthday every year from 10:00 a.m. to 7:00 p.m.;
(3) Child's birthday during odd-numbered years from 7:00 a.m. to 7:00 p.m.

The Mother will also be entitled to the following miscellaneous visitation periods:

(1) Mother's Day of every year from 10:00 a.m. to 7:00 p.m.;
(2) Mother's birthday every year from 10:00 a.m. to 7:00 p.m.;
(3) Child's birthday during even-numbered years.

Appendix D:
Final Order

IN THE CIRCUIT COURT
FOR THE TWENTIETH JUDICIAL CIRCUIT
ST. CLAIR COUNTY, ILLINOIS

In Re The Marriage Of:	)	
	)	
ROSE SMITH,	)	
	)	
Plaintiff,	)	
	)	No.: <u>11-D-123</u>
vs.	)	
	)	
	)	
RICHARD SMITH,	)	
	)	
Defendant.	)	

<u>JUDGMENT OF DISSOLUTION OF MARRIAGE</u>

This case having been called for hearing, and the court having found that the Defendant has entered an appearance in these proceedings and has executed a Marital Settlement Agreement resolving all issues in these proceedings, and the Plaintiff having been present in open court, and the court having heard the testimony of the Plaintiff finds as follows:

1. This court has jurisdiction of the parties to, and the subject matter of, this cause.

2. The Petitioner has been a resident of this state for a period in excess of ninety (90) days immediately preceding the making of these findings.

3. The parties were lawfully joined in marriage on the 1st day of April, 1994.

4. The following child(ren) was/were born to the parties, namely: NAMES AND BIRTHDAYS. No children were adopted. The Petitioner/Respondent is not now pregnant.

5. It is in the best interests of the minor child(ren) that joint custody be awarded to the parties with the Petitioner to serve as Principal Residential Custodian.

6. Grounds exist for the dissolution of marriage in that the parties have lived separate and apart for a period in excess of two (2) years and irreconcilable differences have caused the irretrievable breakdown of the marriage; the parties' efforts at reconciliation have failed and future efforts at reconciliation would be impractical and not in the best interest of the family.

7. That the parties have entered into an agreement concerning the custody and visitation of the minor child(ren), and that this Joint Custody Agreement shall be made a part of this Order and that all provisions of said Agreement are hereby expressly ratified, confirmed, approved and adopted into the Order of this Court.

8. That the parties have entered into an agreement concerning the division of marital property, marital debts and marital assets, the division of non-marital property, that there be *no maintenance* and providing for the support of the minor child, and that this Marital Settlement Agreement is fair and is not unconscionable and shall be made a part of this Order and that all provisions of said Agreement are hereby expressly ratified, confirmed, approved and adopted into the Order of this Court.

THEREFORE, IT IS ORDERED, ADJUDGED AND DECREED:

A. The bonds of matrimony existing between the Plaintiff and Defendant are hereby dissolved.

B. Except as herein provided, the parties are each barred from asserting against each other any claim of any nature, whether for maintenance, formerly known as alimony, for homestead, inheritance or any other alleged right, title or interest.

C. The court has approved the Marital Settlement Agreement entered into by the parties and the terms of that Agreement are hereby made the Order of this court the same as if they were set forth herein verbatim. Failure to abide by the terms of the Agreement may result in a finding of contempt and the imposition of sanctions, including the payment of the other parties' attorney's fees.

D. That the Joint Custody Agreement entered into between the parties is made a part of this Order and that all provisions of said Agreement are hereby expressly ratified, confirmed, approved and adopted as the Order of this Court to the same extent and with the same force and effect as if said provisions were in this paragraph set forth verbatim as the Judgment of this Court. Furthermore, each of the parties hereto shall perform under the terms of said Agreement.

E. The parties shall execute and acknowledge upon the effective date of this Judgment, good and sufficient instruments necessary or proper to vest the titles and estates in the respective parties as provided in this Judgment. Thereafter, at any time, from time to time, both parties shall execute and acknowledge any and all documents which may be necessary and proper to carry out the purposes of this Judgment and establish of record the sole and separate ownership of the property of the parties in the manner herein provided. If either party hereto for any reason fails to execute such documents, then this Judgment shall, and it is expressly declared to, constitute a full and effective present transfer, assignment and conveyance of all rights in this Judgment designated to be transferred, assigned and conveyed and a full, present and effective relinquishment and waiver of all rights herein above designated to be relinquished and waived.

F. This court expressly retains jurisdiction of this cause for the purpose of enforcing each and every term and condition of this Judgment.

G. The Plaintiff's maiden name of _____ shall hereby be restored to her.

Dated this ___day of _____, 201___.

_____

JUDGE

ABOUT THE AUTHOR

Stan R. Weller is a practicing attorney in the Southern Illinois/Metro East St. Louis area. He established the Weller Law Firm in 2006 after a number of years in private firms, as well as a period with the Illinois Attorney General's office working in the Sexually Violent Persons Unit. He received his Bachelor of Science degree from the University of Wisconsin, Madison in 1992 and his Juris Doctorate degree from the Southern Illinois University of Carbondale in 1998. He is a certified mediator, arbitrator, and guardian ad litem, but concentrates his practice in the areas of family law and bankruptcy.

Mr. Weller is a member of BASIL (Bankruptcy Attorneys of Southern Illinois) and has been a featured speaker at the annual BASIL conference. He is also a member of numerous other legal and professional organizations.

Mr. Weller was a contributing author to *Understanding the Effects of BAPCPA: Leading Lawyers on Examining BAPCPA Changes, Adopting New Filing Strategies, and Analyzing Consumer Bankruptcy Trends.* Aspatore Books (Thomson Reuters), 2010.

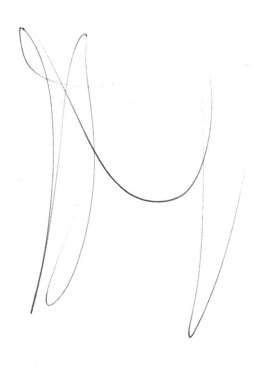